Scrimshaw Techniques

With Gallery of Contemporary Artists

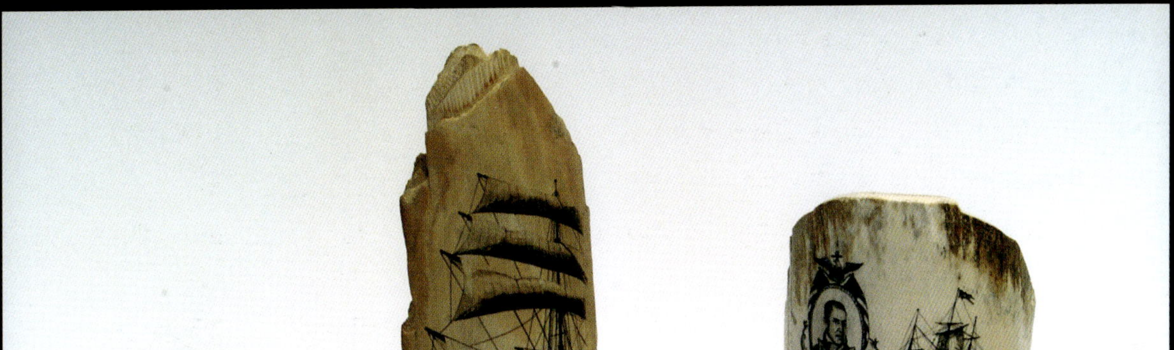

Jim Stevens

4880 Lower Valley Road Atglen, Pennsylvania 19310

Other Schiffer Books on Related Subjects
10 Patterns for Carving Whales. Brian Gilmore.
Carving Dolphins and Whales. Dale Power.
Nautical Antiques. W.D. Ball.
Scrimshaw: The Whaler's Legacy. Martha Lawrence.
Whale Carving. Réal Cloutier.
Whales and Seals Biology and Ecology. Pierre-Henry Fontaine.

Copyright © 2008 by Jim Stevens
Library of Congress Control Number: 2007940404

All rights reserved. No part of this work may be reproduced or used in any form or by any means—graphic, electronic, or mechanical, including photocopying or information storage and retrieval systems—without written permission from the publisher.
The scanning, uploading and distribution of this book or any part thereof via the Internet or via any other means without the permission of the publisher is illegal and punishable by law. Please purchase only authorized editions and do not participate in or encourage the electronic piracy of copyrighted materials.
"Schiffer," "Schiffer Publishing Ltd. & Design," and the "Design of pen and ink well" are registered trademarks of Schiffer Publishing Ltd.
Type set in Futura Med BT/Aldine 721 BT

ISBN: 978-0-7643-2831-2

Printed in China

Schiffer Books are available at special discounts for bulk purchases for sales promotions or premiums. Special editions, including personalized covers, corporate imprints, and excerpts can be created in large quantities for special needs. For more information contact the publisher:

Published by Schiffer Publishing Ltd.
4880 Lower Valley Road
Atglen, PA 19310
Phone: (610) 593-1777; Fax: (610) 593-2002
E-mail: Info@schifferbooks.com

For the largest selection of fine reference books on this and related subjects, please visit our web site at
www.schifferbooks.com
We are always looking for people to write books on new and related subjects. If you have an idea for a book please contact us at the above address.

This book may be purchased from the publisher.
Include $3.95 for shipping.
Please try your bookstore first.
You may write for a free catalog.

In Europe, Schiffer books are distributed by
Bushwood Books
6 Marksbury Ave.
Kew Gardens
Surrey TW9 4JF England
Phone: 44 (0) 20 8392-8585; Fax: 44 (0) 20 8392-9876
E-mail: info@bushwoodbooks.co.uk
Website: www.bushwoodbooks.co.uk
Free postage in the U.K., Europe; air mail at cost.

Dedication

Dedicated to my children, their children, and all future artists.

Acknowledgments

I wish to thank my wife, Mary, for her eternal patience, Sandra Brady and Sara Conklin for their suggestions, J.T. Stevens for his photography, and Sara Whitney for her expert editorial skills.

Disclaimer

Most of the items and products in this book may be covered by various copyrights, trademarks, and logotypes. Their use herein is for identification purposes only. All rights are reserved by their respective owners.

The text and products pictured in this book are from the collection of the author of this book, its publisher, or various private collectors. This book is not sponsored, endorsed or otherwise affiliated with any of the companies whose products are represented herein. This book is derived from the author's own independent research.

Because engraving and associated work on any materials inherently includes the risk of injury and damage, this book cannot guarantee that the information in this book is safe for everyone. For this reason, this book is sold without warranties or guarantees of any kind, expressed or implied, and the publisher and author disclaim any liability for any injuries, losses, or damages caused in any way by the content of this book or the reader's use of the tools and materials needed to complete projects or processes presented here. The publisher and author urge all artists and craftspeople to thoroughly review any project and to understand the use of all tools and materials before beginning any project.

Contents

Introduction 6

What is Scrimshaw? Brief History of the Art Form 7

Basic Questions and Answers 9

Scrimshaw Equipment 13

The Scrimshaw Canvas 22

Cutting, Sanding, and Polishing 37

Care of Ivory and Miscellaneous Tips 42

Making Your Own Handles and Points 45

Getting or Creating the Image 48

Scrimshaw and Inking the Ivory 55

Inlays and Basing 85

In Conclusion 95

Appendix A: Resources and Appraisals 96

Appendix B: Certificates and Affidavits 98

Appendix C: Scrimshaw Gallery 102

Appendix D: Artist Contact List 159

Bibliography 160

Introduction

A word on scrimshaw before we begin.

While collectors do appreciate the potential investment value of scrimshaw, that is not usually their primary reason for acquiring it. The handcrafting of scrimshaw is part of American heritage and each unique piece represents heirloom art passed down from generation to generation. It links us to our past and our rise from cave art to modern masterpieces. It also connects us to the extinct creatures that our ancestors once lived alongside.

Scrimshaw has the combined allure of history, fine art, and heritage. Maybe all of this is what collectors feel when they look at modern scrimshaw. No other art form in America has a longer history. No other expression of art has such significance or influence on the American spirit.

The information in this manual will give you what you need to know to get started in the art of scrimshaw, but read the entire manual before actually starting any of your own scrimshaw. Steps and information in one section are further explained in others and you'll need the complete knowledge to do a good job. I recommend that you read the entire manual before attempting to scrimshaw.

You don't have to be a great artist to learn scrimshaw. This manual was written for the beginner whose background or experience with art may be small, but, scrimshaw is like any other art form in one respect – the more you practice, the better you'll get. Don't be discouraged if your first attempts don't measure up to the high-end scrimshaw you see being done by professionals. My first pieces were no masterpieces, to be sure! But I kept at it, and so can you.

One thing in your favor is that scrimshaw doesn't take a lifetime to learn or become good at. Before you know it, you'll be creating pieces that you can take genuine pride in.

I wish you good fortune!

—Jim Stevens
The Scrimshaw Studio

What is Scrimshaw? Brief History of the Art Form

What is Scrimshaw?

Scrimshaw is a word caught up in controversy. Many say it comes from an old English nautical slang expression meaning "to waste time." But others have supported origins for the word that range from America to China. While the word's origin may always be debated, archeologists have discovered art work comparable to American scrimshaw that dates back to at least 100-200 AD in North America, long before sailors of the 1800s popularized and actually gave name to the art form. Not wanting to simply discard the teeth and bones of land and marine animals hunted for food, native cultures in North America, and the Yankee sailors who followed, invented a style of art that would later come to be known as Scrimshaw, one of just a handful of truly original American art forms. While other cultures around the world certainly worked in ivory and bone, the style of North American cultures and the Yankee whalers were uniquely their own, making scrimshaw a traditionally American art form.

The art of scrimshaw may be generally described as the engraving, carving or fashioning of primarily ivory and bone (but today may also include other natural and man-made materials) into works of art or other decorative or useful articles.

A scrimshander is a person who creates works of scrimshaw.

Brief History of the Art Form

Archeologists have found works comparable to American scrimshaw made from land and marine ivory and bone in North America that date back as far as 100-200 AD, but it was the Yankee whalers of the 1800s who are actually credited with inventing the art form.

With long periods of time on their hands between one whale and the next on what could be as much as three years or more at sea, Yankee sailors took up the art form as a way to pass the time. But at sea, the only ivory and bone available to them were from the whales they hunted. This nautical expression of the art soon passed from ship to ship and it wasn't long before scrimshaw was practiced by whalers and sailors from numerous countries around the globe. Hence, scrimshaw has forever after been associated as an art form started and practiced by whalemen, sailors or others associated with nautical pursuits.

The ivory that sailors used was from the teeth of the whales they hunted. Ivory, whether from land or marine animals, is actually the teeth of these animals. Even the tusks of elephants or the long unicorn horn of the narwhale are actually giant teeth. The ivory teeth of the sperm whale were the forms of ivory most used by sailors. The bone most used by sailors for scrimshaw was from the jawbone of the whales they hunted.

But not all whales have teeth. Actually, most whales have baleen in their mouths instead and have no teeth at all. "Whalebone," as it was called in the days of whaling, is not bone, but is instead baleen, which is composed of keratin, the same substance which forms fingernails. Baleen straining plates, which hang in the mouths of baleen whales, are used to strain water out of their mouths and leave "dinner" behind after gulping huge mouthfuls of water and krill.

But basic to the art of scrimshaw is ivory, and for that sailors used the teeth of the sperm whale and tusks from the Arctic walrus. However, as they sailed the globe they found other sources of ivory that they would trade for. In Africa they traded for elephant, hippo, and warthog ivory. In the Arctic, they traded for mammoth and mastodon and narwhale ivory. In Indonesia and the surrounding islands, they obtained ivory from the babirusa, a type of hog similar to the African warthog.

While many sailors practiced scrimshaw, not all the scrimshaw they produced was quality art. Most was made for trade purposes or for the family back home. But there were a few true artists among the whalers and their work is much sought after today.

Over subsequent years since the time of whalemen, true artists discovered the art form and fell in love with the American style of this ancient craft. But unlike the whalemen of old, responsible scrimshanders today no longer work in ivory from endangered living species, using instead ivory from the long extinct mammoth and mastodon or other legal sources that do not ecologically impact modern species. Modern scrimshanders use only a few pounds of this valuable and beautiful ivory each year, taking great care to avoid wasting even the smallest piece. There simply is no profit in working in illegal material. The legal risk and ecological impact are simply not worthwhile or honorable.

In the early 1970s, the center of focus for quality American scrimshaw shifted from New England to a small town in the northwestern part of the United States. In 1973, Pat Gallery and David Becker formed the Alaskan Silver & Ivory Company (ASI). Their aim was to promote scrimshaw jewelry using fossil ivories. ASI closed down in 1980 but at its peak it drew about 165 workers and artists to ASI's hometown of Bellingham, Washington, and it was these artists who started what has become known as the "Bellingham School" of scrimshaw.

It was a modern renaissance in scrimshaw. It was there that scrimshaw departed from the traditional look of the whaling era and took on the qualities of fine art. Scrimshaw suddenly took on new realism, color, dramatic use of black inks, design sense, and a wide range of subject matter that had never been tried before. In fact, the art started in Bellingham was so different from the scrimshaw of two hundred years earlier it is said the Bellingham artists added an entirely new style to American scrimshaw. It is also the Bellingham style that attracts most collectors to scrimshaw today.

Both early and modern American styles of scrimshaw are still practiced by master scrimshanders today and their work is highly sought after and collected. Perhaps the most noted collector was President John F. Kennedy, who even displayed many of his most cherished pieces in the Oval Office of the White House.

The greatest masters of the craft to have ever picked up a scribe are working today, and though their numbers are few, their techniques and the modern-day masterpieces they create have contributed greatly to the increasing collector's value of this significant and historical American art form. This is the era of the finest masterpieces ever produced in scrimshaw.

Basic Questions and Answers

Okay. Before we get into the actual identification, properties, and the working of ivory, there are a few things you should know.

Read through the following questions and answers so you can intelligently respond to those who will certainly ask you questions. Also, the following information can help keep you out of legal trouble or ending up with faux ivory when you thought you were getting the real thing.

There is also a wealth of just plain good-to-know general information in this section.

Isn't ivory illegal?

The answer is both no and yes. This is because ivory carries different levels of restriction depending on the type of ivory, when it was collected and the controls placed on it within individual countries and by C.I.T.E.S.

The international trade in wildlife and plants is regulated by the Convention on the International Trade in Endangered Species (C.I.T.E.S.). C.I.T.E.S. is a multinational arm of the United Nations. Formed in 1973, the aim of C.I.T.E.S. is to establish worldwide supervision over plants & wildlife that require protection due to declining populations. Headquartered in Switzerland, C.I.T.E.S. delegates meet every two years to review data and set new quotas to increase, decrease or maintain the level of protection of individual species. C.I.T.E.S. regulations do not control a country's internal commerce, only the international trade between member nations.

When shipping ivory products from within the U.S. to outside the U.S., all oosik, walrus, fossil walrus, hippo or warthog ivory require a U.S. issued re-export permit. Elephant ivory is not exportable. Mammoth and mastodon ivories do not require a permit.

Within the United States, wildlife product commerce is regulated on both a state and federal level.

Interstate commerce of wildlife products protected by the U. S. Endangered Species Act of 1972 is regulated by the Dept. of the Interior's U.S. Fish & Wildlife Service (USFWS). Interstate commerce of wildlife products protected by the Marine Mammal Protection Act of 1972 is administered by National Marine Fisheries Service (NMFS).

Check with your own state's wildlife officials so you know your state laws before buying wildlife products for resale within your state. To find out about your state's wildlife laws, contact your state Fish & Game Department's Law Enforcement Division. Have them mail you a copy of their regulations and then read them carefully. Don't trust an agent's verbal remarks over the phone. Information can often be incredibly inaccurate or wildly misinterpreted when accepted verbally.

What are the current levels of ivory restrictions within the U.S?

–Prehistoric mammoth and mastodon ivory are completely legal and carry no restrictions. In the U.S., anyone can dig up mammoth and mastodon ivory as long as they have a permit and the material comes from non-archeological sites.

–Modern wart hog, hippopotamus, and elk "whistler" ivory (the top two canine teeth) are also unrestricted.

–Modern (or white) walrus ivory is generally less than a hundred years old. Recently collected walrus ivory can only be purchased from a native Alaskan and the ivory must also have some form of native work on it, carved or scrimshawed. It is not legal for non-native Alaskans to collect, buy or sell any unworked fresh walrus ivory. The exceptions to this are tusks with a copper tag attached that have a serial number on the tag. These tusks are from an Alaska state culling program from the 1960s and they are legal to buy, sell, and trade across state lines in their natural, unworked form as long as the tag is there.

–Fossil (fossilized) walrus ivory generally ranges from 300 to 3,000 years in age and is most often excavated from the Alaskan permafrost in August and September of each year. Only native peoples are allowed to dig for fossil walrus ivory on their lands. Once purchased from them it can be sold and resold across state lines without restriction. It is typically stained a brownish color.

–Ivory from African elephants can no longer be imported into the U.S. per the African Elephant Conservation Act enacted in 1989 and a subsequent "CITES" treaty; however, any elephant ivory already within the US prior to June 9, 1989 is legal to buy and sell across state lines.

–The sale of whale teeth and bone are tightly restricted. According to The Endangered Species Act of 1973 and USFWS officials, any sale or offer to sell whale teeth or bone carries a $12,000 fine – per act – and possible imprisonment. All other marine mammals and their body parts are considered protected under the "Marine Mammal Protection Act," and similar restrictions apply. The legal sale of sperm whale teeth falls into the following three categories according to articles of The Endangered Species Act of 1973:

1) Antique – is any tooth that has been determined to be 100 years old or older, dating back from 1972 (1872 or older). This ivory is legal to buy and sell across state lines in any form.

2) Pre-Act Teeth – are teeth that date from 1872 to 1972 and are covered by a U.S. government exemption certificate. These teeth are legal to buy and sell if they are accompanied by a U.S. government exemption certificate, but cannot be shipped across state lines in their raw form (they must be carved, engraved or scrimshawed).

3) Any other teeth that were in the country prior to 1972 and not covered by an exemption certificate – These teeth must at the very least be accompanied by a notarized statement from the seller stating that they were in his/her possession, in this country, prior to the 1972 moratorium. These teeth cannot be sent across state lines for commercial resale. The scrimshander must buy these teeth, work on them, and sell them only within his/her state of residence and then only if such purchase and sale is legal under the laws of his/her state.

Here are the actual exemption texts for sperm whale teeth as found in The Endangered Species Act of 1973:

SEC. 10

(f)(1)(A)(ii) any finished scrimshaw product, if such product or the raw material for such product was lawfully held within the United States on December 28, 1973, in the course of a commercial activity.

(B) The term "scrimshaw product" means any art form which involves the substantial etching or engraving of designs upon, or the substantial carving of figures, patterns, or designs from, any bone or tooth of any marine mammal of the order Cetacea. For purposes of this subsection, polishing or the adding of minor superficial markings does not constitute substantial etching, engraving, or carving.

(f)(6)(D) No person may, after January 31, 1984, sell or offer for sale in interstate or foreign commerce, any pre-Act finished scrimshaw product unless such person holds a valid certificate of exemption issued by the Secretary under this subsection, and unless such product or the raw material for such product was held by such person on October 13, 1982.

Under paragraph (h)(1)(A) titled CERTAIN ANTIQUE ARTICLES. – The above restrictions do not apply to any article which is not less than 100 years of age.

–The only completely illegal ivory at the present time is Indian elephant. This animal is considered highly endangered because there are few to none left in the wild. They are almost totally zoo or circus-bred animals, or are domesticated beasts of burden in India.

How do I tell if something is made of ivory, bone or an ivory substitute (plastic or resin)?

Ivory is actually the natural tooth of an animal. Teeth continue to grow throughout an animal's lifetime and as a result, they have a noticeable structure and "growth lines" (called Schreger lines in elephant ivory). Look at the piece carefully under a magnifying glass. Under a 10x magnifier, elephant and mammoth ivory will have visible striations or grain that often show up as diamond or "V" shapes or cross-hatching on the surface or edges of polished ivory. Bone lacks such "V" shaped striations. Under magnification bone usually shows minuscule circular or oval-shaped dots on cut surfaces. These dots are the tiny vessels that once supplied the living bone. Also, all bone exhibits grain-like parallel striations and usually has dark flecks of dirt particles caught in the pores of cut bone – all not present in ivory. Resins or plastics have a uniform surface, usually with no striations or diamond or "V" patterns, however some manufacturers are now introducing faux ivory with an attempt to reproduce some of these features.

When looking at a piece, check the bottom or sides for the diamond or cross-hatch pattern typical of real ivory. Then check again for a slight wood-grain pattern, this is also typical of real ivory. Next, check the feel. Real ivory should have a cool-to-the-touch feeling. Resins or plastics may duplicate one or some of these features, but none duplicates them all.

Also, color often varies slightly (I emphasize slightly) throughout natural ivory (more variable in mammoth) from a creamy white to a creamy yellow-tan or a creamy, light yellow-brown, whereas bone and plastics are either consistent in color throughout, or their color variations may be extreme, especially in stained or colorized resins and plastics.

Later, I will cover specific types of ivory and their individual identifying characteristics. For now, we will examine general methods for determining ivory from other materials.

The next test involves using an inexpensive black light which you can find at most department or home improvement stores. Shine the black light on the piece. Ivory develops a beautiful natural patina with age, which shows up as a yellow-brown overall color under normal lighting conditions. Under ultraviolet light, where the original ivory surface shows through the patina, the ivory will show up a bright white or sometimes a bright white with a slight blue tinge. When ultraviolet light is shined on resin or plastic ivory substitutes, the ultraviolet light is absorbed and they exhibit a dull appearance. (The light emitted by many long wave ultraviolet radiation lamps is hazardous to the eyes. NEVER look directly into a UV light.)

You can also take a Q-tip, dip it in alcohol, and rub the piece in an inconspicuous area. If the patina comes off and colors the Q-tip, chances are good it's a paint or varnish or some other substance that was applied to give the impression of age.

There is one other way to tell if a piece is ivory or plastic, but be aware this should be used only as a last resort since it can be a destructive test, especially to plastic. It is the "so-called" hot pin test. Take a pin and heat it in a flame. Touch the hot pin to an inconspicuous area of the piece. If it is real ivory, nothing much will happen. It may, however, produce a tiny, smooth scorched point (which is never good for the resale value of a genuine ivory piece). If, on the other hand, it is resin or plastic, the needle may melt into the surface and produce a "burr" or small rough spot (never something a seller of fakes is actually going to allow you to do). But if you are very close when you touch the pin to the piece, what you will notice most is the smell of burning plastic. The "hot pin test" is actually more myth than practical. No seller is going to let you touch a hot piece of metal to real ivory and a fraud won't let you do it to their plastic either.

For more information on this topic, you can check out the U.S. Fish and Wildlife Service website. They have many web pages devoted to identification, including diagnostic features and photos.

Why do scrimshanders use real ivory instead of ivory substitutes?

Substitute or faux ivory is made from plastic, and plastics are far from environmentally friendly. They are not biodegradable, and they use scarce petrochemical resources. As far as resources used, responsible scrimshanders only use materials that come from:

–Extinct animals, i.e.: mammoth and mastodon (and fossilized walrus);
–Materials naturally shed by animals, i.e.: antlers and walrus teeth;
–Materials taken from animals long ago, i.e.: piano keys, pool balls, etc.;
–Materials taken annually by legal hunting or by fish and game officials, i.e.: elk "whistler teeth;"
–Materials that do not violate any Federal or State laws

When working with substitutes, micarta will often chip when scratched instead of producing a fine line and it grays with inking, corian doesn't hold ink or pigments well, and ivoryite fails in all areas for scrimshaw work. Vegetable ivory or the "tagua nut" is good for carving, but the natural oils resist ink and other pigments.

What materials other than ivory do scrimshanders work on?

Scrimshanders work on a variety of materials other than ivory that do not endanger living species.

They use naturally-shed antler from deer, elk, and moose for unique collector pieces such as pen bases, letter openers, key rings, fireplace sets, cribbage boards, chandeliers and lamps, and more. Antler is tougher than ivory and is also used for knife scales, handles, and other pieces that get a lot of wear. They also use tagua nuts, a vegetable ivory, to make small unique pieces of jewelry, small game board pieces, etc. Horn, particularly cattle horn, is also scrimshawed. Horn scrimshaw is most often seen on black powder hunting horns. Some extremely hard woods, like ebony, can lend themselves to scrimshaw if properly sealed before work begins. Scrimshaw has even been done on the back of plastic dinner spoons, though these will probably never become "collectable."

While other materials may lend themselves to scrimshaw, it is ivory that holds the real value to collectors and artists alike.

How is scrimshaw made?

Mass-produced scrimshaw is usually photo-transferred, or it may be mechanically painted, laser cut or otherwise mechanically etched into the surface, or, as in the Far East, produced by a workshop of people, each one doing just one part of the work and then passing it off to the next worker who does their part, then the next, and so on.

Museum and collectable quality scrimshaw is done by an individual artist, start to finish. Their individual technique is recognizable throughout the piece. The ivory must first be worked to a fine polish in the area where it will be scrimmed. Polishing seals the surface and keeps pigments that are added later from staining the material in unwanted areas. Some artists then draw designs freehand onto the surface while others first draw on paper and then transfer their design to the surface.

However they start, the next step is to incise the surface of the material with fine scratches or thousands of small holes (called stippling), using sharp tools such as a steel scribe or hobby knives or sharp needles held in a pin vise. Many scrimshanders make their own tools for this task. Some scrimshanders use a modern mechanical device similar to a modified tattoo artist's tool rather than work by hand. Such a tool can greatly decrease the time it takes to produce a piece, but many scrimshanders as well as collectors prefer the look and distinction of a handcrafted piece.

Next, pigment is applied and removed from the surface, leaving behind color in the scratches or holes. It is the unique way scrimshaw is shaded and the "inking" that makes a picture come to life on the surface of the material.

How are finished scrimshaw or ivory sculpture pieces cared for?

Scrimshaw should be treated in most ways just as any fine jewelry, but it also has some unique care requirements.

The scribed picture is permanent, but wear and some substances can remove the pigment or damage or stain the polished surface and even remove fine lines in some cases. Also, ivory acquires a natural yellow-tan patina (coloration) over time. This patina greatly adds to the value that a piece commands and should not be removed during cleaning or restoration.

Do not get ivory unnecessarily wet. The pigments, especially colors, may fade or be removed entirely.

Keep ivory out of bright sun as it dries the ivory and can cause "checks" (cracks) to develop. Sun can also fade certain colored inks and other pigments.

Soap, detergents, shampoo, heavily chlorinated water, and especially jewelry cleaning solutions dull the ivory surface and will also remove the pigments and can even eat away some of the fine scrimmed lines. Some jewelry cleaning solutions not only remove the pigments, they also leave a horrible stain in the ivory surface that cannot be removed.

Most dirt and oils can be removed by simple dusting or a gentle wiping with a clean, soft cotton cloth. Stubborn dirt can be removed with a cotton swab moistened in rubbing alcohol and wiped gently over the surface. Whatever you do, DO NOT SCRUB! A rough scrubbing can remove pigment from fine lines.

While not always considered necessary on properly dried ivory, you can use a light coat of warm beeswax rubbed gently and carefully on the ivory once or twice a year to preserve its look. In lieu of warmed beeswax, a quality paste wax can also be used as long as it has no additives or you can use a product from England known as "Renaissance Wax." If you do wax your ivory, it should be repeated whenever the ivory is cleaned, as any alcohol used in the cleaning will remove it. Waxing gives ivory a shine that many collectors find appealing.

Treated with care, scrimshaw is a valued piece of art – an heirloom to be passed on for future generations to enjoy.

Can old scrimshaw or ivory sculptures be re-inked or restored?

Yes, if it's real ivory. Faux ivory and vegetable ivory don't restore well.

Re-inking, re-etching, and restoring pieces, including mending cracks and broken or missing parts, is also possible in the hands of a master scrimshander/restorer. In the hands of an amateur, restorations are often so poorly done that the restoration itself ends up devaluing a piece.

Also, keep in mind that responsible scrimshanders will not restore or work on whale teeth or other marine mammal ivory (except fossil walrus teeth) without copies of the required paperwork stating that the ivory was legally obtained.

Re-inking should never be done on works of historic value. Re-inking can actually destroy a historic piece, along with its value to history.

Scrimshaw Equipment

Basic Scrimshaw Equipment

You can buy "Scrimshaw Kits" on the market today that include a scribe for making scrimshaw. Unfortunately, the scribe that comes in virtually all of these kits is nothing more than a needle stuck in a piece of wood, with no way to replace the needle when it gets dull and is no longer useful. If you want to create quality scrimshaw, you need the right tools. For really fine work, you especially need tools that will allow you to do stippled scrimshaw. This is because stippling allows for finer detail and shading than traditional line scratching techniques. But use your own judgment when buying tools and only buy what you think you'll really need *after* reading this manual completely. There is no sense spending money on something you probably won't need or use.

What follows are what I consider the scrimshander's "essential" tools. Some items you may already own.

This stuff actually all fits on a very small table and you can find it at any hardware, jewelry supply, and/or arts and crafts store. I'll explain the what/how/why/when of using everything in later chapters.

1. Double-ended pin vise (usually just referred to as a "pin vise"): One end should have a "zero" minimum capacity. A double-ended pin vise allows for holding both needles and small drill bits.

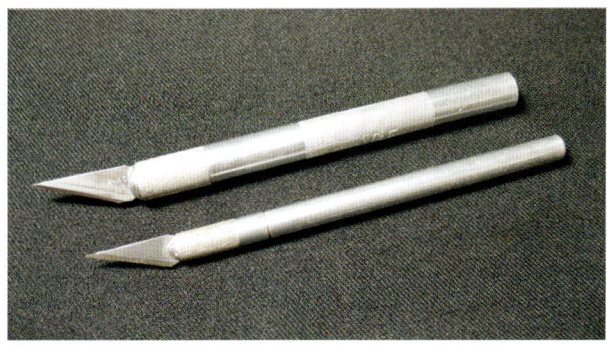

2. Hobby knife (X-acto or other brand) with #16 and/or #11 triangular blades (these are used for scribing lines as well as for cutting all sorts of unexpected things).

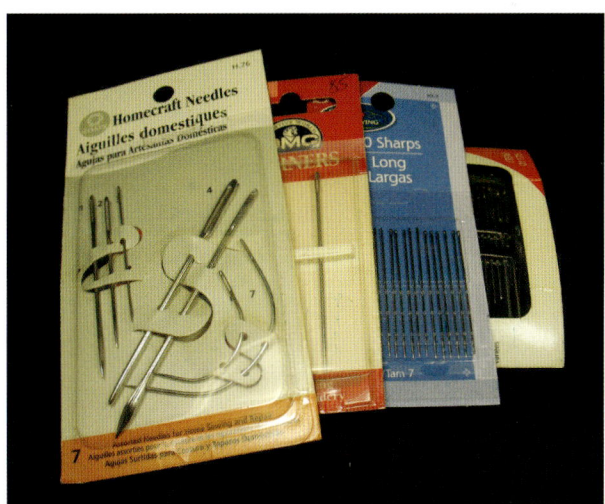

3. Selection of hand sewing needles for use in the pin vise: The needles create the stippling (holes) for your artwork. I use extremely fine point hand sewing needles. You don't need to, but I have also made a large selection of homemade steel scribe points from old broken drill bits that I regularly use for my art and re-sharpen myself. I also made my own comfortable holders for these homemade scribe points. These homemade handles and points are described in more detail in a later section.

4. A few small drill bits that will fit in the pin vise: These are used for drilling various sized holes for jewelry findings, etc.

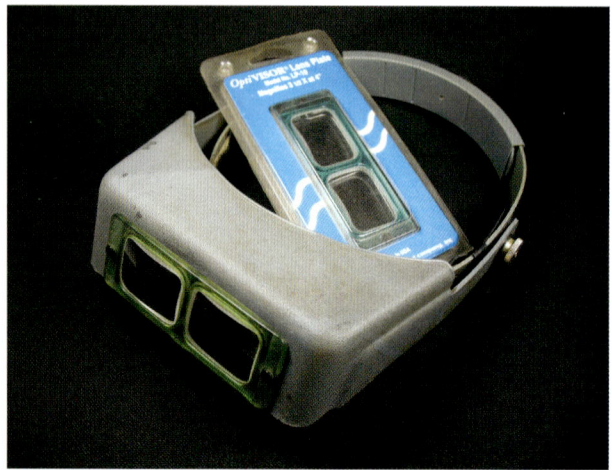

5. Ivory Black or Lamp Black oil paint, or black India ink (such as Koh-I-Noor #3080-6), or black oil-based block printing ink (such as Speedball's), and lightfast, hi-density permanent watercolors if you plan on doing color scrimshaw. (I prefer oil paint for traditional black work. It's not as messy as ink.)

6. Visor style headband magnifier (such as an Opti-visor) that leaves both hands free and allows for 3-dimensional vision. This is a lot cheaper than buying an expensive microscope. Opti-visors come with a choice of lenses. Lens powers are designated by the numbers 3-5-7 & 10. A #3 lens is 1x magnification and allows you to work about 14 inches from your material. Not much bending, but frankly not much help either. A #5 is 2x magnification and allows you to work about 8 inches from your material. I find this is good for most work. A #10 gives 3x magnification but only about 4 inches of work distance. This is great for minute details but can be hard on the back over long periods of time. I use a #5 Opti-visor lens for general work and switch to a #10 for those times when I need the extra power for very fine details. (I must admit, though, that I also own one of those very expensive microscopes.)

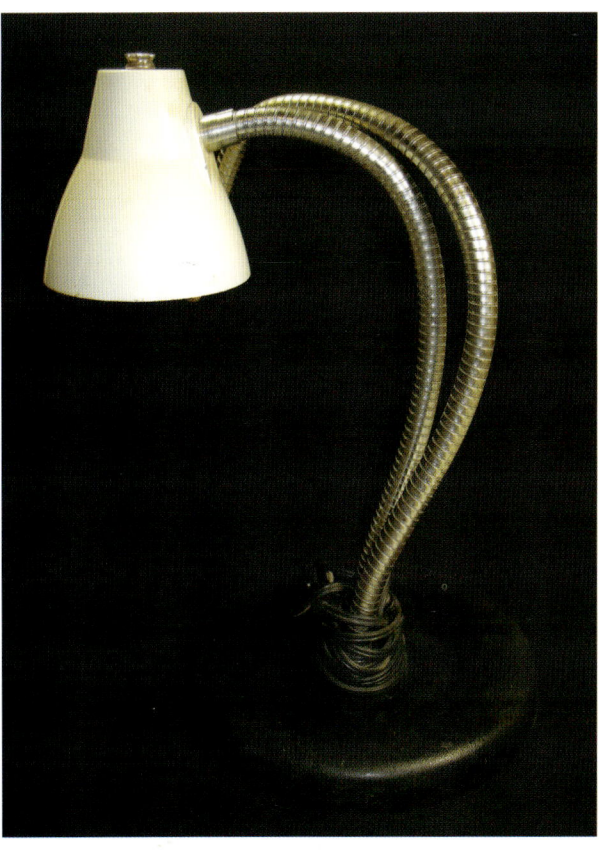

7. A small lamp with a flexible neck and strong bulb for maintaining good lighting around your work as you go. The flexible neck is a real plus when trying to get the light exactly where you want it on your work.

8. A package of cotton swabs (Q-tip or other brand) and a box of toothpicks: These are handy for applying ink.

9. A block of Diamond White or Fabuluster: These polishing materials are best used with a buffing wheel to create a mirror finish on your ivory, antler or other materials. You can buy them at jewelry supply stores. You can actually substitute a quality paste wax (as long as it has no additives) or even toothpaste for final polishing if you're really in a bind and need a temporary replacement.

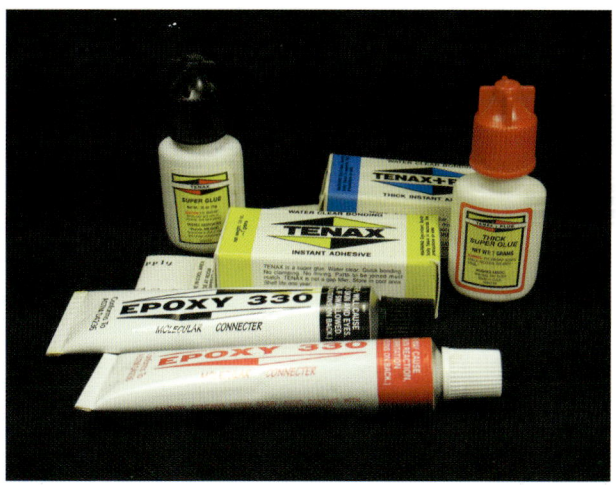

10. A good quality cyanoacrylate glue (Super Glue), watch crystal cement or two-part epoxy (such as Hughes Epoxy 330): I prefer using quality, name brand cyanoacrylate glues for my work. I have used lesser-known brands but have experienced poor results. Cyanoacrylate glue is essential for filling cracks and porous areas and for attaching jewelry findings and holding ivory to almost anything, even inlays. The other glues I've listed are glues I use in special situations when cyanoacrylate glue just isn't appropriate.

11. A small block of stiff modeling clay: I use this behind extremely thin pieces of ivory or other material to prevent it from cracking under stippling pressure. The clay is also useful for holding very odd shaped pieces securely when working on them.

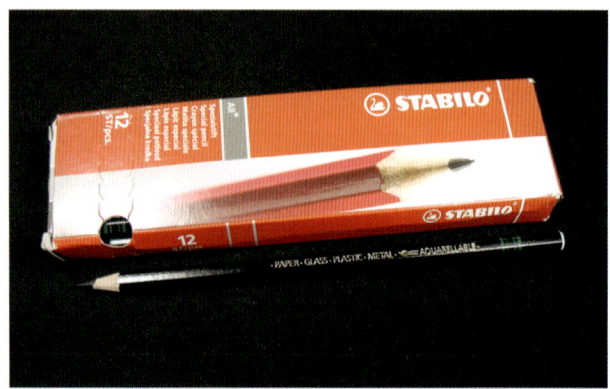

13. A black Stabilo pencil (also known as an aquarellable pencil) for drawing on ivory: This is a water-soluble pencil that will mark clearly, densely, and legibly on any transparent, glazed surface (acetate, glass, metal, photo, film, etc.). Just moisten the pencil tip slightly and it will write on virtually anything.

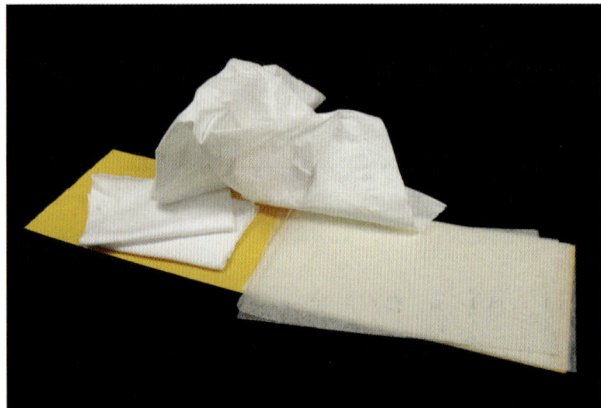

12. Facial tissues, lens cleaning paper, or soft cotton rags for removing ink, wiping cyanoacrylate glue away when filling cracks and for wiping tears from your eyes when you've made a huge mistake. (It happens.) The cotton rags are also good for last minute touch-up polishing.

14. Small can of spray adhesive.

15. Small can of artist's spray fixative: Also referred to as "workable fixative."

17. Small sharpening stone for keeping needles and points sharp while working.

16. Small bottle of rubbing alcohol.

18. Small package of .0000 steel wool and a few sheets of #220, #320, #400, and #600 wet/dry sandpaper.

Additional Scrimshaw Equipment

The following items are what I consider "nice to have" equipment. You don't need them, but they are handy if you have the room for them and plan to do a lot of your own heavy-duty work like cutting and sanding: (You can usually purchase this equipment second hand to keep expenses down.)

NOTE: When using power tools, always wear safety glasses and follow safe operating procedures for each tool. Also, when scribing with needles or other sharp points, always wear eye protection of some kind. A needle or point tip could snap and send the broken piece flying toward your face.

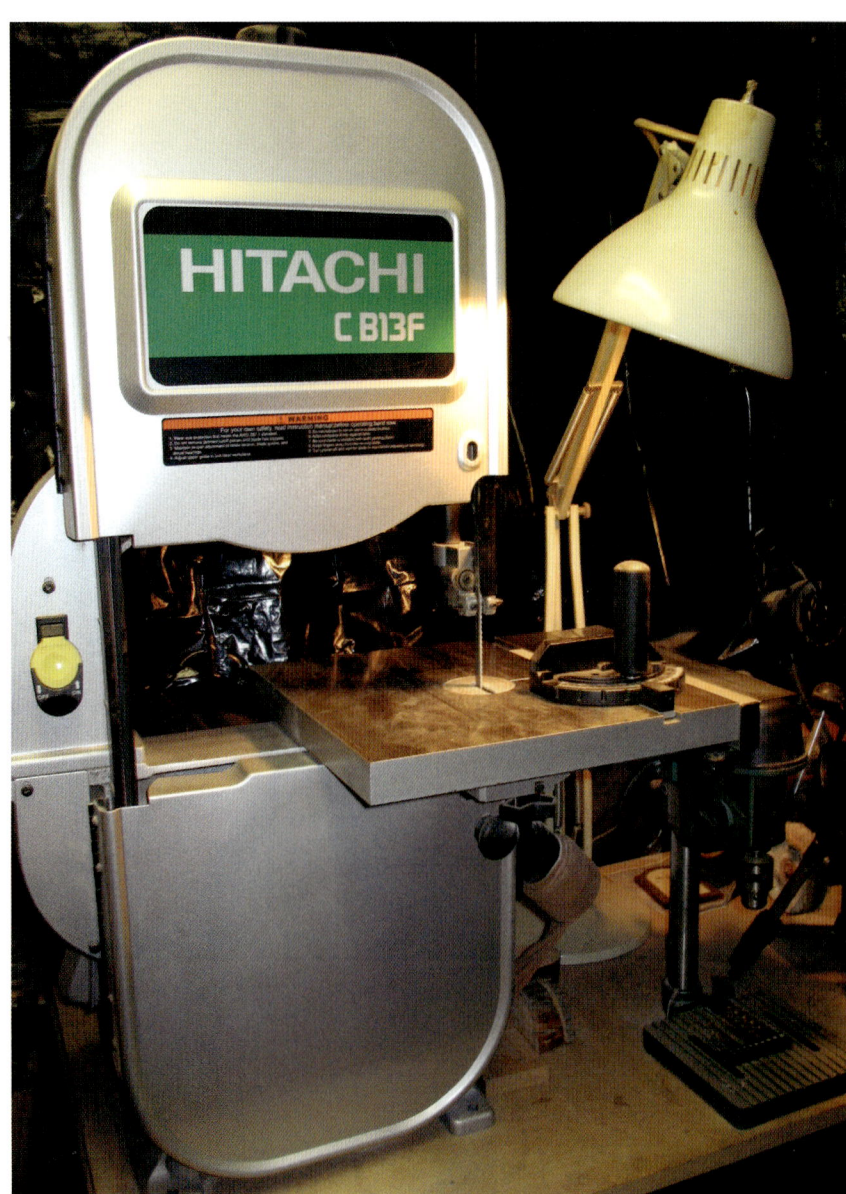

1. A tabletop band saw: (I have both a 9 inch, and 12 inch saw. I also have different sizes of regular woodcutting saw blades that I change out for either heavier cuts or more intricate detail work.)

2. A tabletop bench grinder with a grinding wheel on one side and a buffing wheel on the other side: (I actually have two bench grinders. One just for grinding and shaping materials and one that I use only for polishing.) A two-speed machine is extremely useful for polishing ivory at slower speeds and metal at higher speeds. A 6" x 1" sewn muslin wheel works well for polishing ivory.

3. A tabletop belt sander with multiple grades of sanding belts: One thing I've noticed is that heavier grit belts not only remove more material faster, they also tend not to heat up the ivory or other material as fast as a finer grit belts.

4. A Dremel or Foredom rotary tool with various size bits: I use a Foredom with foot pedal speed control. This tool is great for carving out inlays, drilling holes, shaping wood, and sharpening scribe points. The Foredom is a bit more industrial than a Dremel. I've had mine for years and it still works like a champ.

5. A peg clamp: This is a hand vise with small steel pins and multiple holes for the pins to be moved around in for holding odd-shaped pieces when sanding and polishing. (It really saves the fingertips when working on the belt sander. I know this from painful experience!)

6. Engraver's Block: This is a VERY expensive and not altogether necessary piece of equipment, but I love mine. It acts not only as a simple vise for securely holding any material thickness or shape while doing scrimshaw; it also does double duty with its many attachments as a fully adjustable vise for holding any awkward or curved ivory or jewelry piece that come into my studio for repair. It has proven invaluable as the third hand I was born without.

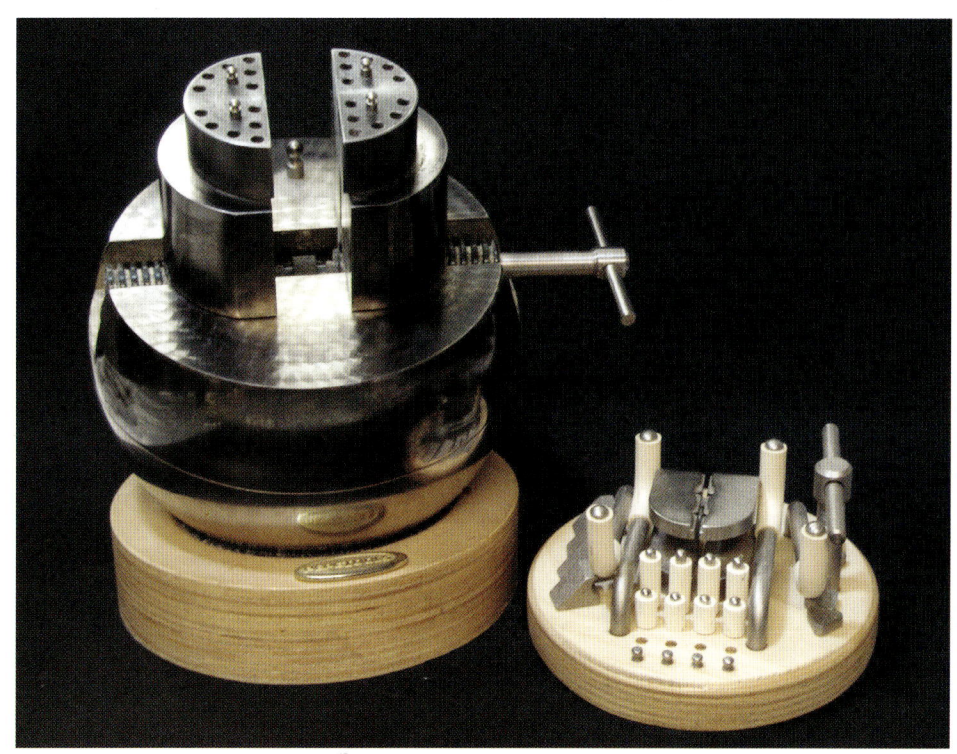

21

The Scrimshaw Canvas: Types of Ivory, Natural Alternatives, and Man-made Substitutes

If you're serious about wanting to learn scrimshaw, then you should know how to identify the material scrimshaw is traditionally and most often accomplished on. It will not only help keep you out of legal and ethical trouble by being able to identify the type of ivory you're looking at, it will also help you understand the characteristics of the material and what to expect once you start your work.

Always check with local officials to determine what laws and restrictions may impact your purchase of different types of scrimshaw material and the subsequent sale of your work. Also, keep in mind the ethical concerns that surround any material you might use.

There are responsible dealers who sell ancient fossil ivory as well as certified modern ivories that are legal to own, scrimshaw, and re-sell. If you are going to work on ivory that must be certified, make sure you get a proper receipt and copy of the certification. Pass a copy of the receipt and certification on to the buyer of your work. Also, take a copy of any paperwork documenting your ivory to any place you display your art. Having it with you could save you inconvenience from well meaning but misinformed individuals.

Here is a list of types of ivory, nature's non-ivory alternatives, and man-made substitutes along with individual characteristics of each type of material.

Types of Ivory

Elephant Ivory

Elephant ivory, though strictly regulated, is still legally available in limited quantities for use in scrimshaw and other work. This type of ivory tends to be softer than walrus, hippo or whale ivory and, in my experience; it is more uniform in how it reacts to scribing, stippling or carving than other types of ivory, especially mammoth. Also, I've come to discover that the whiter the elephant ivory, the softer it is and the easier it is to work – except when working on the end grain of a piece. On an end grain, the exact opposite is true. With end grain, the whiter, the harder. ("Soft" is a relative term! Most people who simply handle ivory would probably never think of any ivory as "soft.")

Elephant ivory is typically a slightly yellow, creamy white color. Over a long period of time, it will turn caramel or yellow-tan in color. This yellow-tan color is called a patina and actually adds to the value of a piece. If you sand or chemically remove the patina from ivory, you usually lessen its value.

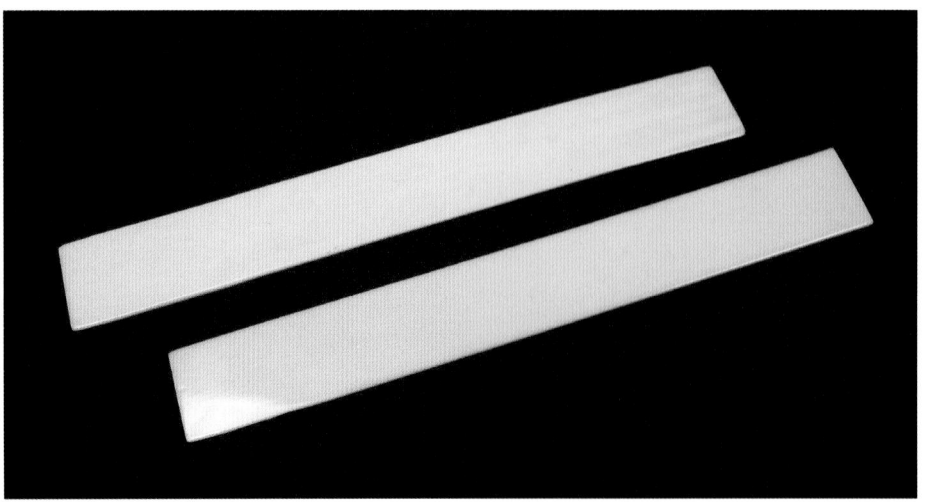

Old piano keys are recycled antique elephant ivory. The long part of the key is called a "tail" and the wide part a "head."

In crosscut view, elephant ivory has a unique wood grain pattern of Schreger lines and often has tinted rings. The whitest cuts of elephant ivory are created when a tusk is cut lengthwise. But not all elephant ivory is creamy white. It does vary somewhat in coloration and grain pattern depending on the type of elephant and geographic region the tusk came from.

When choosing slabs or scales, especially for knife handles, try to select two pieces that were cut directly opposite one another so that any exposed end sections will have mirrored grain patterns.

If you should come across a complete or nearly complete tusk, be aware that tusks over 4 or 5 inches in diameter often have a crack that runs down the inside center of the tusk, usually from the hollow of the tusk to within a few inches of the tip. This is good to be aware of when cutting but is especially important to watch for if the tusk or a large section of it is intended for carving.

If elephant ivory has been allowed to dry too quickly, tusks and large sections will appear "ringed" with checks (cracks) that run in concentric circles along the piece. It is difficult to find and cut suitable pieces from ringed elephant ivory for use in scrimshaw. The checks usually do get smaller and narrower the deeper they run into the ivory, but any crack will still show badly when you ink a piece of work. You may actually be able to work certain checks into a design, or you could take the time to fill certain hairline cracks to make a piece usable, or you may even find a few workable slices without checks from such a section or tusk, but don't pay top dollar for "ringed" elephant ivory.

The outer layer, or "bark" surface, of elephant tusks often have unique grain patterns and swirls with beautiful patinas, all caused by naturally occurring wear. Bark ivory of all types is often highly sought after by knife makers for the beautiful grips that can be made from it.

Walrus Ivory

Before you start thinking about cutting a walrus tusk into slabs for scrimshaw, be aware that the center section of a walrus tusk is full of pores, folds, and tiny cavities which renders slabs cut from walrus pretty much useless for scrimshaw without filling or sealing. An intact tusk, however, is usually fine for both scrimshaw and carving. Walrus teeth, although small, take scrimshaw very well and can also be cut, especially on the diagonal, to expose unique grain and color patterns.

Since trade in walrus is under Federal restriction, I will limit my look at this material to fossil walrus, which is legal for scrimshaw. Make sure you purchase fossil walrus from a responsible dealer who can certify the ivory as legally obtained and not in violation of Federal restrictions.

Fossilized walrus tusk and teeth are found on beaches, on the ocean bottom, and in other places the animals once lived. It is also found in places once inhabited by humans, since early man used walrus tusk for many things, including sled runners, fire starters, fishing net weights, ice axes, scrapers, and other utensils.

Fossil walrus tusk is usually intensely colored from mineralization and the outer layer is almost always weather-beaten, worn, beautiful, and full of hairline checks. Under the mineralized outer layer, often a clean layer of ivory can be found on most pieces that is suitable for scrimshaw.

Crosscut slab of walrus ivory showing typical hairline cracks around the edges and central grain pattern.

Because the natural beauty of fossil walrus is highly prized, scrimshanders will usually not re-cut or reshape a fossil tusk, only polishing an area just large enough for their work, blending their work edges into the natural beauty of the rest of the tusk. Also, since the mineralization process is not uniform throughout a tusk, its colors can range from shades of blue, brown, and gray to even pink depending upon the conditions the tusk was exposed to over the years. It's important to note that collectors prefer the more highly colored fossil tusks.

"Oosik" is the walrus penal bone and this ivory material is often used for knife handles and other "handle" type projects. It is seldom used for scrimshaw since it is very cellular and porous and difficult to scrimshaw without ink settling into unwanted areas.

Fossil Walrus Tusks. *Courtesy of Oso Famoso.*

Fossil Walrus Teeth. *Courtesy of Oso Famoso.*

Hippopotamus Ivory

Hippo ivory may be beautiful, but you'll need a lapidary wet grinder before you can even think about doing scrimshaw on it. This is because hippo tusks are covered in a thin but tough dentine material that is so flinty hard it can even strike sparks from steel. It will destroy any tool you try to use on it unless you've removed the outer dentine layer first.

Because hippo teeth are notorious for being filled with cracks, and because they are small in size, scrimshanders usually polish and use the entire outside of a tooth for a single piece of work rather than taking a chance on cutting a tooth and ending up with crack-filled scrap. Also, if any of the outer dentine is still on a tooth when you try to cut it, your band saw blade will be ruined before you even have time to shut it off.

Hippo teeth have essentially three shapes – curved and blunt, conical and pointed, and the largest is crescent shaped. Hippo teeth are extremely dense, hard, and very fine grained. In fact, it is difficult to even see the grain in hippo ivory. Also, because hippo teeth are so hard, they take almost twice as long to scrimshaw as other types of ivory.

There is another method for removing the outer

Fossil Walrus Chunks. *Courtesy of Oso Famoso.*

Fossil Walrus Crosscuts. *Courtesy of Oso Famoso.*

using a sharpening stone. The original tip is very fragile and is probably going to break off anyway, plus, the new slightly "rounded" tip you've created, while still giving you a sharp point to cut with, also allows you to turn the tool more easily when following curved lines.

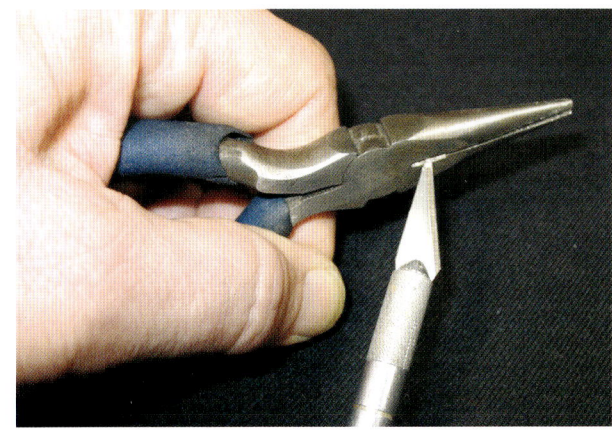

Break off the knife blade tip.

Sharpen and bevel the backside of the tip.

Since cuts using a knife are so shallow, this is probably not the best method of scrimshaw to use when cutting through a paper template affixed to the ivory. The pressure of cutting through the paper is almost too much to maintain good control over how the knife cuts into the ivory. Using a knife, you will have better control over your blade if your image is drawn or traced directly onto the surface of the ivory. An exception to this control problem when cutting through a template is when you're using transparent tape for your pattern. Transparent tape cuts so easily that you should be able to cut through the tape without any control trouble at all.

Shading with a blade is achieved by creating crosshatched lines and/or lines that are cut one alongside the other. The closeness of your lines, or their distance apart, determines how dark or light an area looks to the viewer. Another way to make lines appear heavier is to make V-shaped cuts in the ivory, a technique that will take some practice to master. When trying to create long straight lines, control becomes a problem. Long lines can very easily "wiggle" off-track on you and not look good at all. Try cutting long lines in shorter segments, making sure to start your blade for a new segment of the line exactly where you left off on the previous segment. This method can also be used to maintain good control when scratching long curved or circular shapes as well.

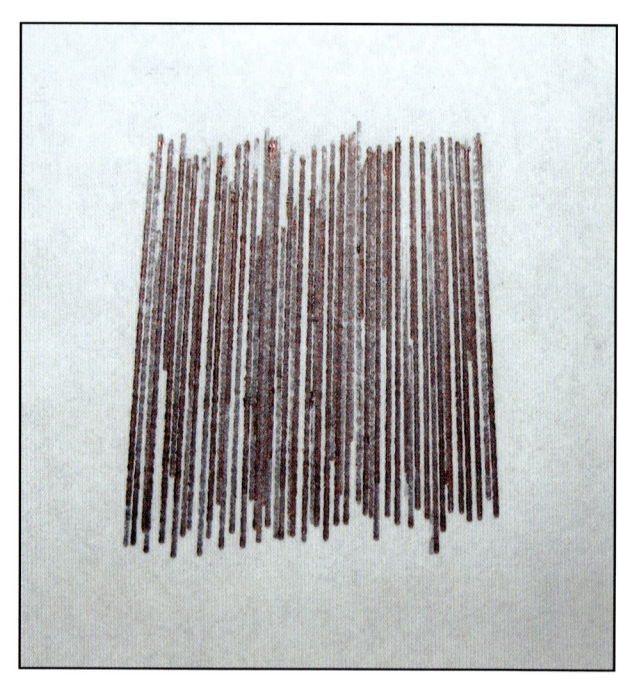

Line shading.

Crosshatching.

Ink frequently as you work. Also, start by outlining everything first and work in stages on shading and details. Working slowly will also prevent lines from being put where they don't belong. If an area ends up too dark, carefully and lightly retracing your cuts can help to remove some of the ink to lighten the area.

When scribing lines with a hobby knife, water is often represented using *horizontal* curving parallel lines of varying lengths and darkness. Clouds are often done using *vertical* parallel lines of varying lengths and darkness above and below a curving base line to create a cloud's many hard and soft shapes.

Cloud lines using a hobby knife.

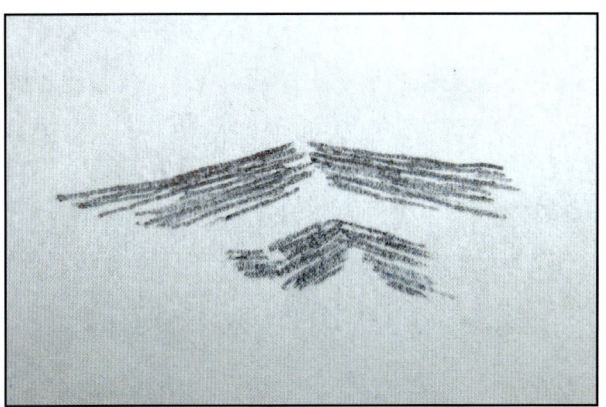

Wave lines using a hobby knife.

Another tip when using a knife in combination with stippling is a trick for creating realistic fur on animal forms. You can use the tip of your knife to make a few small, short strokes that extend outward from the edges of an animal to give the impression of fur that extends past the animal's face or body. A caution, however: It only takes a few of these strokes in a few well-chosen spots to give you the overall effect you need. If you go overboard with too many of these strokes all over the animal, the edges of your furry critter will just look blurry instead of fur-like. You can also leave a small open segment when stippling an animal's outline, then use the short knife cuts through the open spot in the outline to resemble fur extending from the animal's body.

When scribing using a hobby knife blade on a curved or irregular surface, I recommend wearing a leather glove on the hand holding the material. This is for obvious safety reasons. If the blade slips on the surface of the material, you don't want to bleed all over your work.

Regardless of the technique you're using, always work in a comfortable position with your arm supported in such a way that all the scribing motion is generated within the hand to prevent arm fatigue.

Keep your light focused exactly where you'll be placing the point of your scribe or needle. Your lamp will only create one small pool of light on the ivory surface that you'll find perfect for working in. It is because you'll always be working inside that small pool of light you must be able to adjust your lamp if necessary. This is why I recommend a lamp with a flexible neck. At first it might take a while to find the most comfortable position for your arm that also allows you to work inside that perfect pool of light, but once you've found your favorite position for scrimming, you'll just naturally find and work in that same comfortable position forever.

It's also important to consider the contour or shape of the ivory you're scrimming. The flatter the surface, the bigger the pool of light your lamp will create. If the surface is extremely curved or rounded, the pool of light available for working in will be small, and maybe narrow, making your job more difficult. Curved surfaces not only increase the time it takes to complete a design, they also increase hand and eye strain. But despite the added difficulty, work done in the round has its own rewards.

When inspecting your progress before you ink, you may have to tilt the ivory at an angle to see your scribe marks clearly, but at the right angle under a bright light, they will show up even though you haven't added any ink yet.

Here are a few final notes on shading. Heavily shaded areas using a blade are created with many types of cuts, sometimes combined with the stippling technique. Also, multiple cuts to create heavily shaded areas should be slightly offset from one another or cut in different directions as in crosshatching. Don't just use a bunch of random cuts. The shading won't look natural. Also, all shadowing should follow the contours and lines of your image. Make sure your dots or lines follow the flow and direction of the shadowing in an animal's fur or on a building's edges or the rise and fall of a landscape if you want the finished picture to look realistic. One last point I need to make is that if you stipple or cut over one area too many times, you can overwork the ivory and end up with blotchy-looking areas. Heavy shading does take a little care to come out looking good.

While all the techniques I have discussed are aimed at scrimshaw on ivory, remember that the same principles apply to work done on bone, antler, horn, and most other materials. Keep in mind, however, the peculiarities of each material that I discussed in the earlier chapter: "The Scrimshaw Canvas." For example, don't forget that horn has a persistent memory and doesn't like to be pushed around. As a result, you may need to go over your work a second or third time to make the scrimshaw stand out. Also, don't forget that antler has only a thin band under its tough outer covering that is acceptable for scrimshaw, so don't file or sand too deeply when preparing antler for scrimshaw. Just keep in mind the peculiarities of each material you will be working on.

Well, that's about it. Now all you have to do is sit down and get to work! And remember to enjoy as you practice and learn! The next few pages will take you through a start-to-finish project so you can get an idea of the actual steps I go through when completing a mammoth ivory necklace piece.

Centering a drilling mark for a jewelry finding. The ivory oval is sitting on a small metal centering jig.

Scrimshaw Necklace Project – Stippling Technique

After cutting, shaping, and polishing the ivory for a pendant, the next step is to drill a hole near one end of the ivory oval for a jewelry finding. The necklace chain will go through the finding. Findings are the components used to assemble finished jewelry and include such items as bails, clasps, jump rings, headpins, bead caps, earring backs, and hooks. Here are some examples of typical jewelry findings:

Open jump ring.

Post with loop or pearl cup with loop.

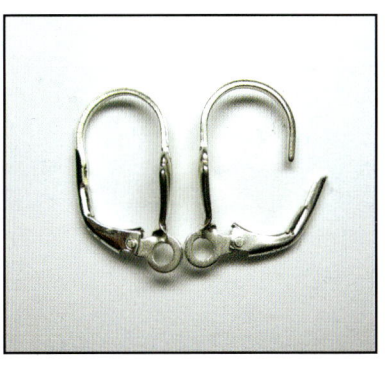

Earring lever back clasp.

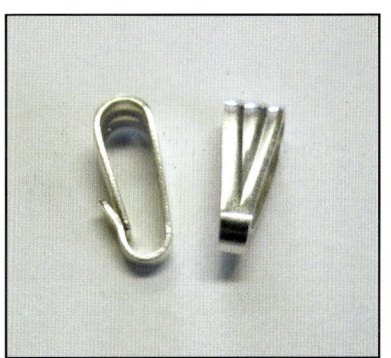

Bail finding.

Findings can be silver, gold, sterling, gold-filled, or made of a base metal, and it seems there are as many different types of findings as there are stars in the night sky. Take some time to better match the findings you will use to the color and shape of your ivory. It is just one of many small details that will help make your work look more professional.

Drilling a hole for the jewelry finding using a hand drill.

After drilling a hole for the jewelry finding, we can see exactly how much of the ivory surface remains for our image. Instead of tracing or drawing an image onto the ivory, our next step for this project will be to use a computer or copy machine to copy a drawing (we'll stick with the tiger theme) and reduce it in size until it fits on the ivory oval in an eye-pleasing manner. The paper image we create is then cut out, sprayed or brushed on the back with adhesive, and then firmly pressed into place on the ivory in the exact location where we want the finished scrimshaw image to be. *Make two copies of your image.* You'll need the second image because your first one will probably be ruined when you remove it from the ivory after your initial outline work. You'll need the second one to refer to as you complete your scrimshaw of the image.

Cut out the paper image.

Place the glued paper image onto the ivory. Make sure there are no bubbles or creases in the paper.

Make sure you have a very sharp needle or scribe point before starting your outlining work. The needle or scribe must be extremely sharp to push through the paper and also leave a mark in the ivory that will actually hold ink. If your needle is the least bit dull, you will do a lot of outlining but have little to show for it after inking the ivory later. Now, with a new needle or sharp scribe point, begin outlining your image. If your picture is of an animal (as our image is) or some other portrait, include the eyes as well as all other key elements and major shadow areas during this initial stage of your work.

Remember! You are doing scrimshaw, not drilling for oil! Even though you are going through paper and then into the ivory, don't twist or otherwise try to drill your dots into place. If you do, you'll end up with a blotchy looking mess once you remove the paper and ink your work. Just push firmly in and out as if the paper was not even there and you will be fine. At this stage of your work, use a medium to medium-light pressure for all the dots you are putting in. You may not have a "feel" for it at first, but very soon you will get that "feel" for how your dots are etching into the ivory through the paper. By the way, heavy pressure when making dots (for darker lines and/or shadows) is something best done after the paper is removed. With the paper out of the way, you are better able to see and adjust your shading as you work. So, at this point, a medium to medium-light pressure is all you really need for outlining.

Most beginners either push too hard or too lightly when outlining. This creates really dark lines or practically no image at all once the paper is removed and the piece is inked for the first time. Not to worry. You will get better with practice and very soon you will be in control of the pressure you apply at different stages of your work.

Outline with a sharp point. Include eyes and all major shadow lines and areas. The ivory is being held in place on an engraver's block, but two hands work just as well.

Remove the paper.

After you have outlined your image, remove the paper, clean the ivory surface and then ink the image and wipe the ink away so you can readily see your work thus far.

Clean the surface.

Next, slowly begin to fill in the rest of the picture while referring to that second copy of the image you made earlier.

Ink the image

Remove the ink.

Initial inked outline. The lines are extremely light and best viewed under magnification.

Begin filling in the rest of the image while referring to your original art. Remember to ink and wipe frequently as you work.

If you feel more comfortable or confident about it, you can actually scrimshaw the entire image instead of just doing an outline when you go over the art for the first time. I like to outline and then do the detail work after the paper is removed, but you need to work the way you feel most comfortable. Remember that since you are using a medium to medium-light pressure on the needle when working through the paper, once it is removed you will need to go over the image a second time to give depth to your shadows, lines and transitions.

Once the paper is removed and you can better tell what you are doing, remember that darker areas require more dots, more closely spaced, and applied with slightly more pressure. The lightly shaded areas require fewer dots, farther apart, using a lighter pressure. Very light but still shaded areas require just the slightest pricking of the ivory surface to give the look you're after, and the very lightest or "white" areas of the image actually have no dots at all. The polished ivory surface acts as the lightest color in the image. Remember, when you need it, going over your dots with a hobby knife can create exceptionally sharp and dark lines. This technique works well to make features such as eyes or lanyard lines on a ship really stand out.

Transitions from dark to light (as in the shading of animal fur) can easily come out looking too dark, too light or otherwise unnatural. Don't be discouraged. With just a little practice, you'll begin to understand what it takes to create really smooth looking transitions that make the eye comfortably follow from dark to light.

Also, remember that once you do remove the paper, ink frequently as you work so you have immediate feedback with regard to your shading, transitions, and the art you're creating with your dots. It is common for me to place a few dots, ink, place a few dots, ink – and so on. Getting in a hurry to put down a lot of dots before inking is the fastest way to a mistake and a ruined piece of work. If you go slow and do it right, the result should be similar to the next image, which shows the tiger we have been working on as a completed piece of scrimshaw jewelry.

This piece is the result of patience and a willingness to ink often as the work proceeds. It is something you can do as well – maybe better!

Finished piece with a sterling silver bail jewelry finding.

Scrimshaw Necklace Project
– Scratch Technique

This project will be completed using a hobby knife, or detailing knife as it is sometimes called. This style of scrimshaw is often referred to as the scratch technique. The best blade for this type of scrimshaw is one with a long bevel. There are a number of different blades and styles you can purchase, but the #11 blade is very well suited to scrimshaw and is the one used in this project.

Before using the knife, I always snip off the very tiny tip of the blade as was explained earlier. After snipping off the tip, it needs to be slightly reshaped using a sharpening stone. Rub each side of the blade at about a 30-degree angle until the tip is slightly chisel shaped. This shaping makes the point similar to an engraver's tool and allows the blade to turn more easily on the ivory or other material as you work. It is especially helpful when following curves.

Remember that shading with a blade is done with line density, crosshatching, v-cuts, and the depth of your cuts. You can even shade with the stippling technique by using the point of the blade to create your dots. The v-cut is a technique that requires a bit of practice to perfect, but once you master the technique, v-cuts can create very bold lines and dark shadowing.

When using the knife, hold it as you would a writing pen and create your lines by pulling the knife, not pushing it. If you push the knife, the blade will dig into the ivory and eventually get stuck or gouge the ivory surface. Pulling the blade is the way to go. Also, control over lines and curves is in your hand, not by moving your arm. If your arm starts moving as you work, you'll discover that your lines will begin to wobble instead of running in the direction you intended. Remember, control is in the hand, fingers, and wrist – not your arm.

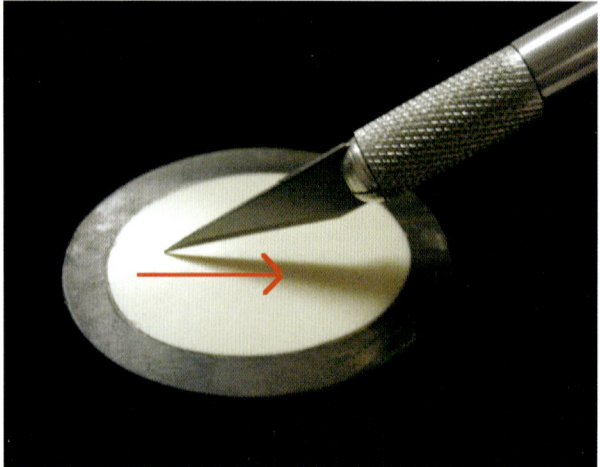

Pull the blade, don't push.

Also, consider using the back of the blade tip as you work. Sometimes turning the blade over gives you better control and better cuts. Also, don't forget that you can use the point of the blade to stipple the image.

Using the back of the blade.

Using the point to stipple.

Our next step is to get our image. We will use a computer printed picture and then transfer it to transparent tape for this project. Because the tape is easier to cut than paper, this method of getting our image onto the ivory allows us to maintain better control of our blade while scrimming the image.

Our first step is to copy our computer printed image on a copy machine. An image directly from an inkjet printer *will not work* for this method. You need a copy machine image.

Next, we need to cut out the image so we can transfer it to the tape.

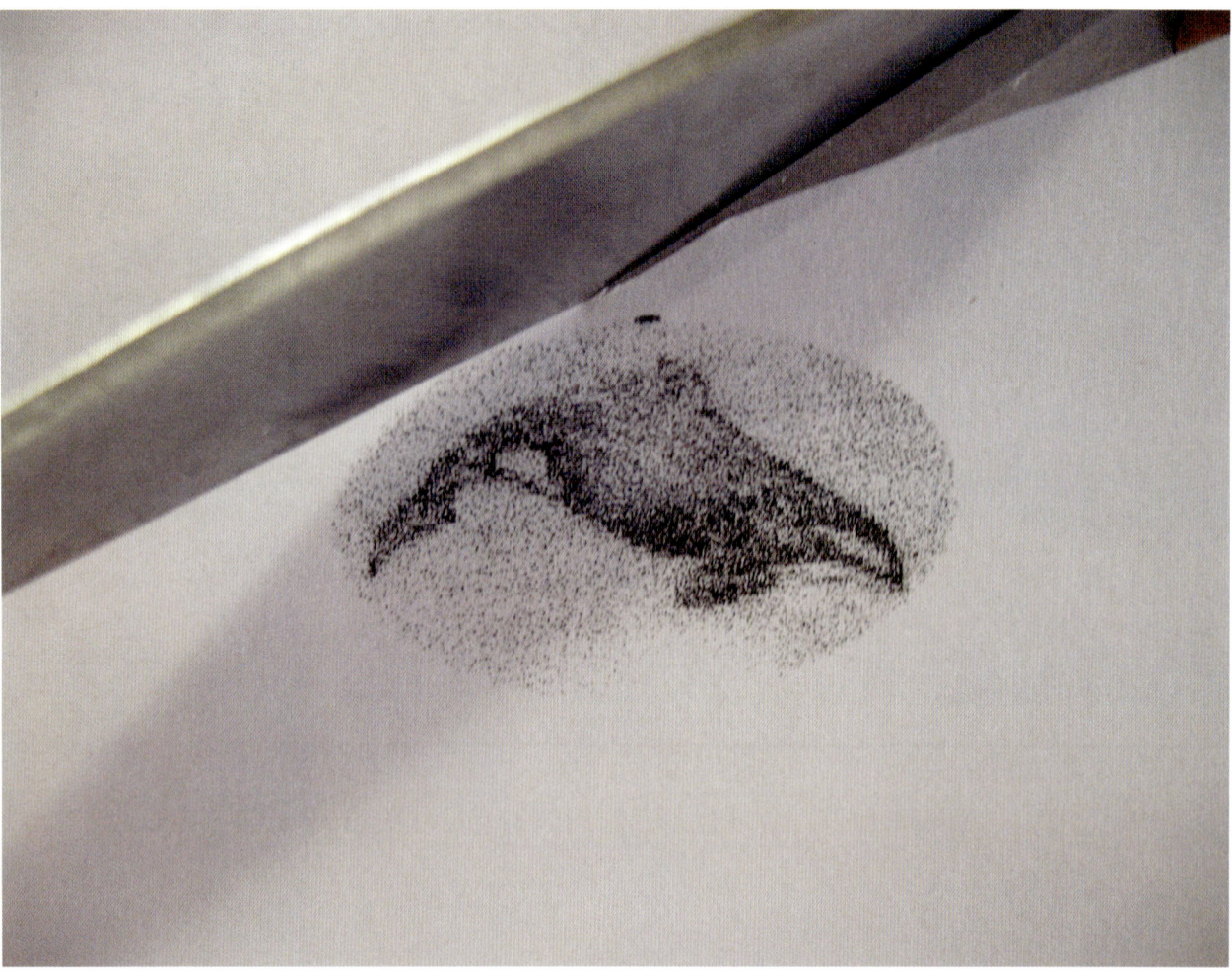

Now press the transparent tape over the image and then burnish the paper down well to the tape.

Press tape over the paper image.

Burnish paper onto the tape.

Soak tape and paper.

The next step is to place our tape covered image in a bowl of water for about 3 to 5 minutes. This softens the paper so we can gently rub the paper off the back of the tape. The paper will be gone, but the image will remain on the tape.

Carefully remove paper from tape.

The tape will still have a certain amount of stickiness which will allow us to stick the tape down onto our ivory. If the tape isn't sticky enough, give it a light coat of spray adhesive.

Tape image to ivory surface.

With our image on the ivory, we can now begin our scrimshaw. Follow the image by cutting along the outline of the image, the eyes if there are any, and cut in the shadow areas using crosshatching or closely spaced lines to insure shadows will be properly dark when the ink is applied. Cutting through the tape is much easier than paper and this allows the knife to move with more control as you work on the image.

After the image has been cut in, remove the tape and ink the ivory. After inking, remove the ink and examine the image to see what areas need more work.

Cut the outline.

Cut lines for shaded areas.

Image on ivory after removing tape.

As you can see, the image looks like a series of rough lines, but that's okay.

Now, begin to fill in different areas with crosscuts and other types of cuts to smooth out the image and create the shading needed for the final look to our image.

As you cut, think about the types of cuts that will help your image the most. Will crosshatching work? What about a few v-cuts? Or maybe even a little stippling with the point of the blade. Ink frequently as you work so you can check your progress.

Filling in light and dark areas.

Ink frequently as you work.

Proper shading begins to show.

After working on the image for a while, you will begin to see how your cuts help the image begin to take shape.

Finished piece.

After you have completed all your cuts, you will have a final image that you can display.

A knife can be very difficult to properly control, but with practice you will get better and better. Keep in mind that the scratch technique is the original way scrimshaw was created by the Yankee sailors. It has a rich history of beautiful work over many, many years.

Inlays and Basing Your Art

In the "Cutting and Polishing" section I referred to using a v-board for cutting intricate designs and patterns in ivory, but I didn't say how to inlay those pieces after they've been cut out. The other thing we haven't discussed yet is how to base, or what sort of stand you can have for your scrimshaw art pieces. We'll now look at the basics of both.

Inlays

Inlay work requires extreme patience and accuracy. The first time you speed up or lose your concentration, I guarantee you'll either cut something wrong or sand something so uneven it's unusable. Again, I speak from hard-learned, tearful experience. And when you're working in materials that are just plain expensive, even in their rough original states, a mistake is also hard on the pocketbook. So work at each step of the inlay process as carefully and as slowly as it requires.

Let's look at a simple inlay project – inlaying an ivory oval into a piece of wood for a necklace. I like to use ironwoods and very black ebony for this. Expensive materials, to be sure, but they make beautiful surrounds for an ivory necklace. There are many other exotic woods out there that would also make beautiful surrounds and you may want to experiment until you find woods you especially like. A good idea is to cut the wood into a square shape at the beginning of this process. Also, cut the wood both wider and slightly thicker than the ivory you'll be using. Later, the ivory and wood will be sanded together as one piece after all the inlay work is done. This will make all the surfaces blend smoothly and seamlessly.

The first thing you need to do is cut and sand the edges of your ivory. Next, cut out your wood block. Now you need to transfer the shape of your ivory oval to the surface of the wood so you can cut out the area where the ivory will fit into the wood. Before you begin, however, label both your ivory oval and your wood with a mark that will tell you which is the front and which is the back of both pieces of material. It gets important later when you're trying to fit the pieces together for gluing. With all the handling, fronts and backs, and tops and bottoms can often become confused and invite mistakes.

Once everything is marked, place a small drop of cyanoacrylate glue on the back of your ivory oval and press it down and hold it where you want it on your wood surface until the glue sets. It's important to use only one small drop of glue because you're going to want to pop the ivory off the wood once you're done transferring the ivory shape. This can be done by sliding a hobby knife blade under the ivory and working it around until the ivory pops free. Too much glue and you'll have secured the ivory to the wood for life. Don't worry about any glue residue on the ivory after it is freed from the wood. It will be sanded off later.

Once the ivory is secure, use a hobby knife blade and cut around the edge of the ivory, pressing firmly into the wood as you go. This cut outline will give you an edge guide for your routing tool or jeweler's saw and also keep the surface of the wood from chipping as you cut or rout up to the edge of this outline later. Keep the hobby knife blade at the same angle all the way around the ivory oval. You want to cut an outline of the ivory into the wood that is consistent all the way around. Also, keep the blade against the ivory all the way around. This insures a tight fit later. Go slow and cut in small sections, keeping the blade against the surface of the wood and the ivory at all times. If you try to cut and turn the piece too fast, you'll end up with a wavy line that occasionally pulls away from the edge of the ivory. This will create an ugly gap later between the wood and the ivory when they are fitted together.

Keep the blade close against the ivory.

Keep the blade at the same angle all the way around.

Now pop the ivory off. It's time to remove the wood inside the outline you've cut. Because the cut line can be hard to see, I use a white china pencil or piece of white chalk and go over the cut line so the white powder gets down into the cut. This way I can see it better while I'm cutting or routing out material. It's an easy way to see when I've reached the absolute edge of my outline so I don't cut or rout beyond it.

Okay, it's time to cut out the oval in the wood. There are two ways to do this – with a jeweler's saw or a straight flute router bit attached to either a drill press or a Dremel tool mounted on a drill press stand. I use both methods depending on the wood I'm using. African ironwood tends to split and shatter under the vibration of a router, so I often use a jeweler's saw for woods that I can't trust under a machine.

When using a jeweler's saw, drill a small hole inside your outline, then run one end of the jeweler's saw blade through the hole and reattach it to the saw. Now saw up to the inside edge of your outline and then follow it around until the wood within the outline is completely cut out.

To rout woods like ebony and others that can handle the vibration, hold the wood directly below the routing bit, pull the handle down, and carefully drill out a hole slightly wider than the bit in the center of the outline. Now turn off the Dremel or drill and lower it down and lock it in place once the bit is centered in the hole and it's cutting height covers the full depth of the wood.

Turn the Dremel or drill back on while holding the wood, and let it rotate to full speed. Holding the wood firmly with the fingers of both hands, turn and move the wood until you have routed all the wood away, nearly but not completely, up to the edge of your outline. Be aware that if you try to rout out too much material too fast, or if your bit is dull, you can get nasty kick backs that will almost tear the wood from your grip. Lastly, rout away that final thin layer of wood you left next to your outline. Routing away a very narrow layer of wood is a smoother process and allows for greater control and accuracy than trying to rout out large amounts of material while also trying to guide on your outline at the same time. This tip will give you a better final fit later. Always follow recommended safety requirements for any power machine.

Using a jeweler's saw on a v-board (bird's beak).

While routing, blow away the accumulating wood shavings often so you can always see where you are. When you get to the final stage of routing – that last, thin edge of wood against your outline – be careful, go slow and be precise. If you get in a hurry, you'll overshoot your line and ruin the final fit of the ivory.

Now take your wood out of the drill press and dry fit the ivory, making sure you match the top of the ivory with the top of the wood. This is why we marked them in the beginning. Look for any areas that are too tight, where the ivory doesn't quite fit. Mark the section that needs to be shaved back a little more and then use a hand file or put the wood back in the drill press and shave off the very slight amount of wood in this section. Try your dry fit again. Repeat this process all around the wood as needed until the ivory oval fits snugly into the cutout. It's slow work, but slow and careful assures a tight, good-looking fit.

Once the ivory dry fits snugly, use your cyanoacrylate glue and run a liberal amount all around the edge of your ivory oval. Press the ivory back into the wood. Quickly turn the entire piece over and press the ivory and wood both down against a piece of paper on your table top (the paper is so you don't get glue on your table). Make sure both the ivory and wood surfaces are flush with one another against the flat tabletop. Don't worry if the ivory and wood stick to the paper. You can lightly sand off any paper residue later. Some scrimshanders use a two-part epoxy instead of cyanoacrylate glue, but I've found epoxy doesn't always penetrate the ivory as well as cyanoacrylate glue for a good hold.

Once this glue has dried, run a bead of glue around the inside of the wood where the ivory and wood meet. This will fill any small areas that the glue may have squeezed out of during the initial gluing process and insure a solid connection between the ivory and wood. You can use a toothpick to insure the wet glue gets down into needed areas. Any excess glue build up will be removed later during your sanding.

   Once the glue has set, determine how wide you want the wood to be around your ivory and mark that oval outline on your wood. Now, cut the wood along your marked line on your band saw (or by hand) so you have an appropriately sized wood surround for the ivory. Cut a little wide since you will sand it down to its final size later.

   Now it's time to sand the back, the front, and the sides. The front and back need to be sanded down until the wood and ivory are level with each other and no glue residue remains. By cutting your wood slightly thicker than your ivory you have the chance to sand the wood down to match the ivory perfectly.

Peg clamp holds odd-shaped pieces.

Using a peg clamp will save your fingertips.

But be careful when sanding: Only sand until the wood and ivory match. This means lifting the piece from your sanding belt often to inspect where you are so you don't sand too far. BE CAREFUL! It is very easy to sand a piece too thin and make it worthless. Once the front and back are level and all residue has been removed, continue sanding by hand with ever finer sandpaper until the ivory is utterly smooth and brilliantly polished as described in the "Cutting, Sanding, and Polishing" section.

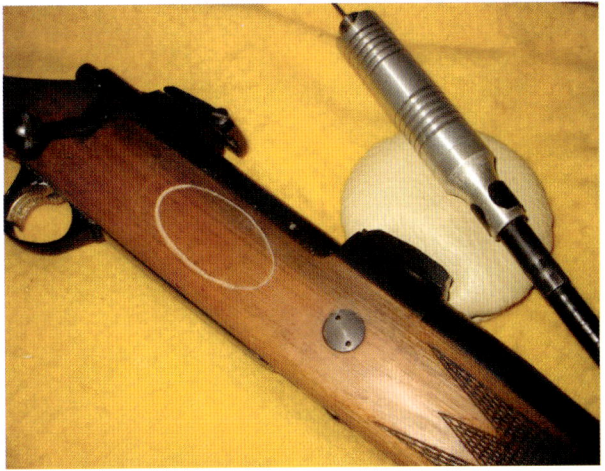 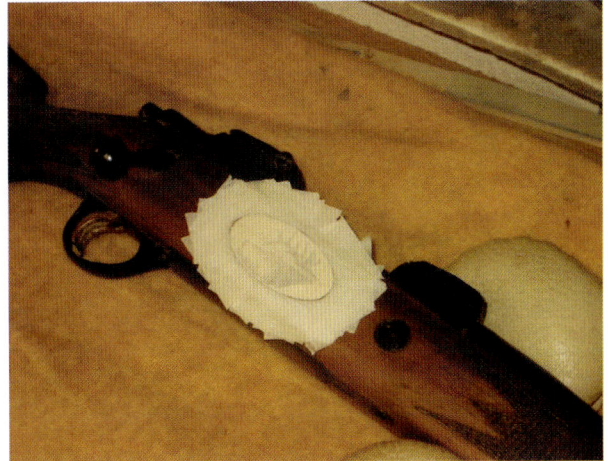

You'll find the wood polishes to a fine finish at the same time as the ivory using this process. With the ivory and wood sanded and polished, you can begin your scrimshaw work. ALWAYS DO ANY INLAY WORK BEFORE YOU SCRIMSHAW! The reason is obvious when you consider all the sanding that is done during the inlay process. Sanding will remove any scrimshaw you've done on the ivory.

Some inlays do not require cutting all the way through your wood to inlay your ivory – as with gun stocks. In these cases you need to set the depth of your routing tool just to the depth needed for insetting the ivory, or you can do the cutting carefully by hand with a Dremel or Foredom rotary tool.

Whenever using cyanoacrylate glue for inlays, cleaning up any glue that squeezes out during the fitting process is often easier after the glue dries, not while it is still wet. A sharp hobby knife can pop hardened super glue loose in big sections. Wiping wet super glue leaves a thin haze of glue that, after it dries, can only be removed by sanding or with acetone. One benefit of any glue you use on inlays is that it acts as a barrier to prevent any natural wood oils from leaching into the ivory and staining it over time.

You'll discover that cyanoacrylate glue will secure small ivory pieces to virtually any other material. Sometimes, as with the backs of bolo tie slides, I will roughen both the ivory and the back of the metal bolo slide before gluing to insure the glue penetrates the ivory and has multiple surfaces on the metal to "grip" to.

Nothing is more embarrassing than to have a bolo tie or other piece of work come apart in the new owner's hands. For inlaying some things, like precious stones into an ivory piece, I use Watch Crystal Cement. It adheres well to the smooth stone and bonds the stone firmly to the ivory. This glue can also be used instead of cyanoacrylate glue for many other projects, if you find you get good results with it.

For gunstock inlays, I start with my cut outline around the ivory just as I've explained before, but then I tape off the area around the cut line to protect the wood. The tape protects the surrounding wood should I slip as I carve out the opening and depth for the ivory with my Foredom or hand tools. It's never happened to me, but it's a scrimshander's worst fear. Always protect a gunstock with thick tape in any areas that may need it. For gunstock inlays I use a glass gel to inlay the ivory. The glassing not only acts as an adhesive, it also acts as a protective backing to help prevent any future cracking of the ivory from the shock of repeated firing.

Basing Your Art

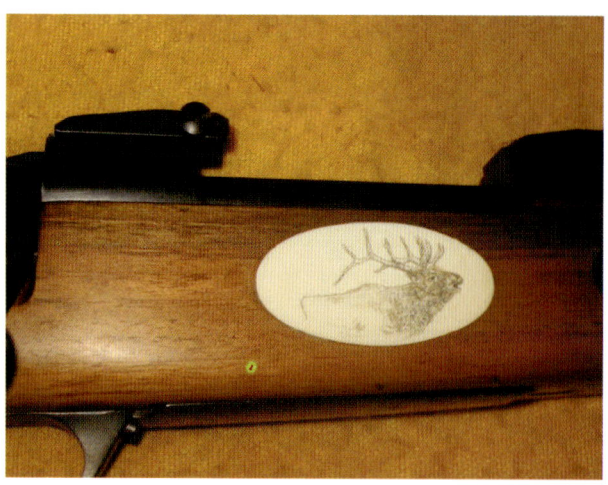

If you want to play with the "pros" of scrimshaw, you need to base or display your art in an eye-catching way. But not all eye-catching bases or stands need to be expensive or time consuming. Sometimes a simple yet bold base is the best way to display a piece of art. I have one simple and cheap display base I have used to display award-winning works of art that I will share with you. In fact, the award-winning pieces were on these cheap bases when they won their respective awards in juried art shows.

Start with a scrap piece of half inch plywood that has one smooth side. Measure out a rectangle (usually seven to nine inches by five to seven inches) and cut it out. Then measure and cut another piece about an inch smaller all the way around. Sand the edges of both pieces until smooth.

Using two half-inch screws, screw the smaller piece to the larger piece matching the rough bottom sides together and making sure the smaller piece is centered on the larger one. If the very tip of a screw passes through the top of the larger piece, find a hammer. Carefully applied, it will easily bash screw tips level with the surface. Next spray paint the wood with black enamel spray paint all around.

Once the paint dries, use a spray adhesive and glue a sheet of twenty pound white copy paper to the top of the piece, making sure it lays completely smooth with no air bubbles. Next, trim off excess paper by turning the piece over and following the edges of the wood with a sharp hobby knife. Turn the trimmed piece back over and spray paint the paper with the same black paint you used before.

That's about it for the basics of inlaying ivory. I've had to inlay ivory into some pretty strange and hard materials in the past. For these harder materials, I've even had to use water-cooled diamond covered drill and grinding bits on my Foredom to cut the inlay areas. I've cut inlays for ivory into everything from granite and marble to a variety of metals. This is very tough, expensive, and exacting work that you may not want to get involved with, especially not right away.

Once the paint dries, you have an eye-catching stand that seems to just barely float in the air and it's a great platform for showing off a piece of scrimshaw art. I often use double-sided cellophane tape on the bottom of the art to make sure it doesn't slide around on the platform.

How simple and cheap is that! And it works great, as evidenced by the fact that I have won first place art show awards with pieces based just this way.

Another way to base your art is inside glass display boxes and domes. You can find a variety of shapes and sizes at hobby shops to fit just about any size art you need to place inside them. One trick I've learned that can make your piece stand out inside these glass enclosures is to glue a cheap square or oval mirror to the bottom of the glass base. You can find these cheap little mirrors at hobby shops. The mirror reflects light upward and gives your work an almost ethereal look that is definitely eye-catching.

Another way to use these glass enclosures is to affix a hooked rod or chain to the top of the glass or buy one that has a hook already in it. Now hang a necklace pendant from the hook or chain inside the glass. This is an eye-catching way for an owner of your jewelry to show it off somewhere in their home rather than keeping the piece hidden away inside a jewelry box.

A traditional way of displaying scrimshaw is on a mount made specifically to hold the piece yet still allowing for the piece to be easily picked up and replaced. Such one-of-a-kind bases are often intricately designed with shell, ivory or stone inlays on their front, side, and back surfaces. They may also have the title of the art piece affixed to the base using small, engraved plates of copper or ivory. The top of these bases usually have specially designed parts that hold the art upright and in place while being displayed.

A majority of well known scrimshanders do not make their own bases. Instead they have bases made for their pieces by master woodcrafters according to a design they provide. This naturally adds to the value as well as the cost of an art piece.

But you don't have to hire out for a quality, eye-catching base. With a little ingenuity you may think of some great, yet inexpensive ways to display your art. Some ways may include shadow boxes, frames, a variety of small pedestal shapes … the ideas are endless and only limited by your imagination. In some cases, I have even carved wood into various shapes that blend with the design of the art to become part of the overall art while also serving as a base for the scrimshaw.

Whatever base you decide on, a base should and will add to the overall appeal of the art and may improve overall sales of your work.

When you can (I know it's not always under your control), also consider the lighting a piece is displayed in or under. Proper lighting can be a huge factor in how a piece appeals to viewers and buyers. Don't neglect lighting when considering how a piece is displayed. If you can, bring your own miniature spotlights. You can find mini-spots at industrial lighting supply outlets and some craft stores. You can position two or even three of these tiny mini-spots to get just the right lighting effect, placing them in such a way that the lights, themselves, are actually ignored by viewers but their effect is tremendous.

In Conclusion

I hope that this manual has given you enough knowledge and encouragement to try scrimshaw, regardless of the amount of equipment or courage you may have to begin the experience. Scrimshaw is the oldest art form in North America and, for me, the most fascinating and enjoyable art form to work in.

With any luck, I've kindled a desire in you to try your hand at being a scrimshander. If so, I need to warn you, there's loads more to learn once you've mastered the skills I've covered in this manual. But you'll enjoy the learning process, believe me.

People accuse me of occasionally stepping outside the traditional concepts of scrimshaw with the way I include multiple inlays, unusual basing, precious stones, copper inlays, etc. in my art pieces, but whose to say you won't be the next innovator? All art forms need a good shot in the arm now and again to keep them fresh.

Remember that the things I have covered are recommendations, not law. As you begin to work and learn, you may find your own way of doing certain things that differs entirely from what I do or teach. That is perfectly normal. While certain things about scrimshaw tend to be universal in nature, I still don't know any two scrimshanders who do everything alike at any given time on a project.

I did not cover powered engraving tools in this manual, which are used today by many professional scrimshanders. This was deliberate because these machines are expensive, require a certain amount of practice to master, and while they may speed up the scrimming process, they are not necessary to produce quality work.

I started out with charcoal and paint as a young artist, then gravitated to bronze sculpture, and finally to scrimshaw. You just never know where creativity will take you. Like me, you just might feel at home with this oldest of American art forms.

Appendix A: Resources and Appraisals

I know a few dealers in legal ivory I trust and respect. The same is true for appraisers of ivory art and scrimshaw. As you widen your horizons in the field of scrimshaw, you may well encounter others with whom you have a good experience. You will want to add their names to this list.

The Boone Trading Company, Inc.
P.O. Box 669
562 Coyote Road
Brinnon, WA 98320
Phone: 800-423-1945
International Calls: 360-796-4330
Web site: http://www.boonetrading.com/
Ivory and other legal wildlife materials as well as materials for jewelry making, educational needs, etc. Accepts credit cards, personal checks, and money orders. David Boone and his folks always work hard to make sure you get exactly what you need.

Oso Famoso
P.O. box 654
Ben Lomond, CA 95005
Contact him by email: oso@osofamoso.com
Web site: http://www.osofamoso.com/
Ivory wholesaler. Accepts personal checks and money orders. No credit cards. Oso is really good at asking a lot of questions just to make sure you get the exact quality of material you need.

Coast Ivory
6100 Hans Road
Moss Point, MS 39562
Phone: 228-475-2877
Web site: http://www.coastivory.com/
Pre-ban elephant, mammoth, walrus, hippopotamus, and warthog ivories, sea shells, and other exotic material. Ken and Kim Harris always seem to have a good selection of bark scales and larger tusk sections.

Knife Scales and Custom Knives
30020 N Stampede Rd.
Athol, Idaho 83801
Phone: 208-683-3835
Web site: http://www.knifescales.com/
The Howe's have a huge selection of knife scales in a variety of materials, including ivory, and their prices always seem very reasonable. The size of ivory knife scales make them great pieces for scrimshaw and especially inlay work. They don't have to be used just for knives.

David Warther Museum / IvoryBuyer.com
2561 Crestview Drive NW
Dover, Ohio 44622
Phone: 330-343-1865
Web site: http://www.ivorybuyer.com/
David is a master carver and his work is brilliant. He buys a lot of pre-banned elephant ivory for his own work, and if he has it, he'll cut your ivory order to your specifications and you'll get excellent material and great service. He checks emails when he's not working so don't freak out if he doesn't answer your email for a couple days. Absolutely great at making sure you get exactly what you need.

Ken Fredericks
MELLO-METAL
2014 James St.
Bellingham, WA 98225
Phone: 360-734-8377
Email: tfgmm@msn.com
Ken is available 10-5 (Pacific time) weekdays or by appointment on weekends. Ken is an ivory supplier, mount maker, repair technician, and appraiser, but most important to him is his work as a mount maker.

The Naja
6810 North Broadway, Unit J
Denver, Colorado 80221
Phone: 888-340-6252 (Toll Free)
Fax: 303-426-8110
Email: naja@najatools.com
Web site: http://www.najatools.com/
Travis Ogden and his crew are the best at finding what you need in the way of jewelry supplies (like findings), equipment, and specialty tools that are very useful for scrimshaw artists. If you call them, they often come up with helpful solutions for your problems that you might not have thought of on your own.

Cutlery Specialties
6819 S.E. Sleepy Hollow Lane
Stuart, FL 34997-4757
Phone: 772-219-0436
Fax: 772-219-7674
Email: Dennis13@aol.com
Web site: http://www.restorationproduct.com/
Supplier of Renaissance Wax. A great product for ivory cleaning, polishing, and preservation.

Sara Conklin, ISA CAPP
International Society of Appraisers
Certified Appraiser, Personal Property
Box 30203
Cromberg, CA 96103
Phone: 800-464-4208
Email: sconklin2@pngusa.net
Sara appraises American whaleman and Alaskan scrimshaw bone and ivory objects, both period and contemporary. Very knowledgeable in the field of ivory appraisal.

International Society of Appraisers
1131 SW 7th St., Suite 105
Renton, WA 98057-1215
Phone: 206-241-0359
Fax: 206-241-0436
Email: isa@isa-appraisers.org

Appendix B:
Certificates and Affidavits

If you're going to buy, sell or transfer certain types of ivory, a Certificate of Exemption, a Certification of Subsequent Seller/Shipper/Exporter, or an Affidavit of Origin may be necessary.

If you purchase an antique or pre-banned whale's tooth, you should expect that the seller will include a Certificate of Exemption for the tooth. If they are a legitimate reseller, they should also include a Certification of Subsequent Seller/Shipper/Exporter. These required federal forms prove that the tooth has been certified as legal for resale and meets the requirements for resale in the U.S.

You might be surprised to know that these forms are not issued by the U.S. Fish and Wildlife Service as one might expect, but are instead issued by the U.S. Department of Commerce for the National Oceanic and Atmospheric Administration.

When you buy pre-banned elephant ivory from a supplier, some sellers (but certainly not all of them) will include an Affidavit of Origin with the elephant ivory they send you. Because these affidavits or certificates are supplied by individual sellers, they may be called by different names by different sellers. Some may send you something they call a certificate, others may call it an affidavit. Whatever the name, it is the seller's assurance to you that the elephant ivory you've purchased is legal pre-banned ivory.

The next pages give you examples of a Certificate of Exemption, a Certification of Subsequent Seller/Shipper/Exporter and an Affidavit of Origin.

The included forms are copies of ones I have actually received. They are copies of a copy and are a bit rough but they give you a look at what these forms actually look like.

NOAA FORM 88-119 (11-76) U.S. DEP...
NATIONAL OCEANIC AND ATMOSF...

CERTIFICATE OF EXEMPTION UNDER P.L. 94-359
RENEWAL OF CERTIFICATE OF EXEMPTION UNDER P.L. 96-159

Issued to:

(withheld)

Period During Which This Certificate is Valid: From 02/17/80 thr...
(unless amended, suspended, revoked or otherwise modified by the Assista...
for Fisheries, NMFS).

COMMERCIAL ACTIVITIES EXEMPTED:

(1) ~~The prohibition as set forth in section 9(a)(1)(A) of the Act, to ex... pre-Act endangered species part from the United States~~; (2) The prohibit... forth in section 9(a)(1)(E) of the Act, to deliver, receive, carry, trans... ship in interstate or foreign commerce, by any means whatsoever and in t... commercial activity any pre-Act endangered species part; (3) The prohibit... forth in section 9(a)(1)(F) of the Act, to sell or offer for sale in int... foreign commerce any pre-Act endangered species part.

PARTS OR PRODUCTS EXEMPTED: Finished scrimshaw products to be made from 2,935 sperm whale teeth and 26 pounds of whale bone.

This Certificate of Exemption is granted subject to the provisions, term... conditions of the Endangered Species Act of 1973, as amended; the regula... issued thereunder; and any subsequent changes in the law or regulations.

_____   APR 8 1980
Assistant Administrator for Fisheries   Date of Issua...

CERTIFICATION BY SELLER/SHIPPER/EXPORTER

Under penalty of perjury, I hereby certify that the endangered species par... products, derivatives or any products containing such parts, products or... accompanying this Renewal of Certificate of Exemption, or otherwise sold,... transported, or shipped in interstate or foreign commerce, and in the cou... commercial activity, under this Renewal of Certificate of Exemption, may ... be sold, delivered, transported, shipped or exported and are the same, or... the same, stock of pre-Act endangered species parts or products registere... this Renewal of Certificate of Exemption with the National Marine Fisherie... Department of Commerce, Washington, D.C. 20235.

_____   3-12-
Signature   Date

(Front)

CODE OF FEDERAL REGULATIONS
TITLE 50 - WILDLIFE AND FISHERIES
CHAPTER II - PART 222
SUBPART B

Certificates of Exemption for Pre-Act
Endangered Species Parts

Section 222.11-8 Subsequent purchaser provisions

(a) Any person granted an exemption, including a renewal, pursuant to this subpart, upon an interstate sale of any exempted pre-Act endangered species part, shall supply a copy of the certificate of exemption as well as a signed written certification to each purchaser that such part may lawfully be sold, transported, or exported pursuant to the terms of an exemption granted under the Act and the regulations promulgated thereunder.

(b) Any subsequent purchaser, unless an ultimate user, shall upon an interstate sale supply a copy of the certification of exemption as well as a signed written certification to each purchaser of such part that such part may lawfully be sold, transported, or exported pursuant to the terms of a certificate of exemption granted under the Act and the regulations promulgated thereunder. An ultimate user, for the purposes of this subsection, shall mean any person who has acquired such endangered species part for his own consumption.

(c) Any incerstate purchaser of pre-Act endangered species parts shall, within 90 days after the receipt of such parts, submit to the Assistant Administrator a written report specifying the quantity of such parts or products received, the name and address of the seller, a copy of the certification supplied pursuant to paragraph (a) of this section, the date on which such parts were received, and the intended use of such parts by the purchaser.

TO BE COMPLETED BY SUBSEQUENT PURCHASERS UPON AN INTERSTATE SALE BY HIM TO ANY PERSON

CERTIFICATION BY SUBSEQUENT SELLER/SHIPPER/EXPORTER

Under penalty of perjury, I hereby certify that the endangered species parts, products, derivatives or any products containing such parts, products or derivatives, accompanying this Renewal of Certificate of Exemption, or otherwise sold, delivered, transported, of shipped in interstate or foreign commerce, and in the course of a commercial activity, under this Renewal of Certificate of Exemption, may lawfully be sold, delivered, transported, shipped or exported and are the same, or part of the same, stock of pre-Act endangered species parts or products registered under this Renewal of Certificate of Exemption with the National Marine Fisheries Service, Department of Commerce, Washington, D.C., 20235.

Signature _____   Date _____

(Back)

DAVID WARTHER MUSEUM

Daytime: 330-343-1865

2561 Crestview Drive NW Dover, Ohio 44622

AFFIDAVIT OF ORIGIN

This document serves as an Affidavit of Origin attesting to the legal pre-act status of the ivory listed below. This ivory is African Elephant (Africana Loxodonta) ivory. It is legal within the United States in accordance with Federal law and regulations 50 CFR section 17.40 e and Section 1533(d) . This ivory is legal within the United States but can NOT be exported to another country under any circumstances in any form as sold, reworked or modified.

Form of Ivory:

__ Trimmings and Offcuts   __ Randall Style Block _____

2 Slabs (Knife ~~or Gun Grip~~) *Large*   __ Tusk Section _____

__ Inlay Slabs   __ Whole Tusk _____

__ Carving Pieces   __ Pair of Tusks _____

__ Piano/Organ Keytop Set   __ Other _____

Area of Tusk Origin: <u>Kenya</u>

Age of Tusk (Year Brought into U.S.): <u>1967</u>

Tusk I.D. Number for Federal Government reference: <u>SCWA 025267</u>

Sold To: <u>Jim Stevens   Wheat Ridge, Co. USA</u>

All tusks are pre-ban and well documented. We work with our congressman and the U.S. Fish and Wildlife Department to document the ivory properly and to keep abreast of the changes in the laws relative to ivory in the United States.

The tusk identification number given above is your reference number for this tusk.

_____   5/2/04
David Warther II - Museum Director   Date

Courtesy of David Warther II

Appendix C: Gallery of Art

DAVID ADAMS

David Adams has maintained a career in scrimshaw since 1979 and has scrimmed on every type of ivory known to mankind. His scrimshaw is displayed in public and private collections worldwide.

103

GAETAN BEAUCHAMP

Gaetan is a prolific knife maker who lives in the northern part of Quebec, Canada. In addition to knife making skills, he is also recognized internationally for his award winning scrimshaw.

Instead of using traditional material such as ivory, Gaetan turned to dark surfaces such as water buffalo horn. The challenge at first was to train his mind to work in reverse. As he puts it, "I had to learn to work with the light instead of the shadows. The concept is similar to that of a film negative. When I first started I had a headache for a week." I think you will agree that his pain was our gain.

All work on a Beauchamp knife is done by Gaetan, with the exception of the sheath. Gaetan's wife, Denise, transforms each piece of leather she uses into an exceptional sheath of superb quality. Her talent is readily evident in the beautiful product she creates for each knife.

105

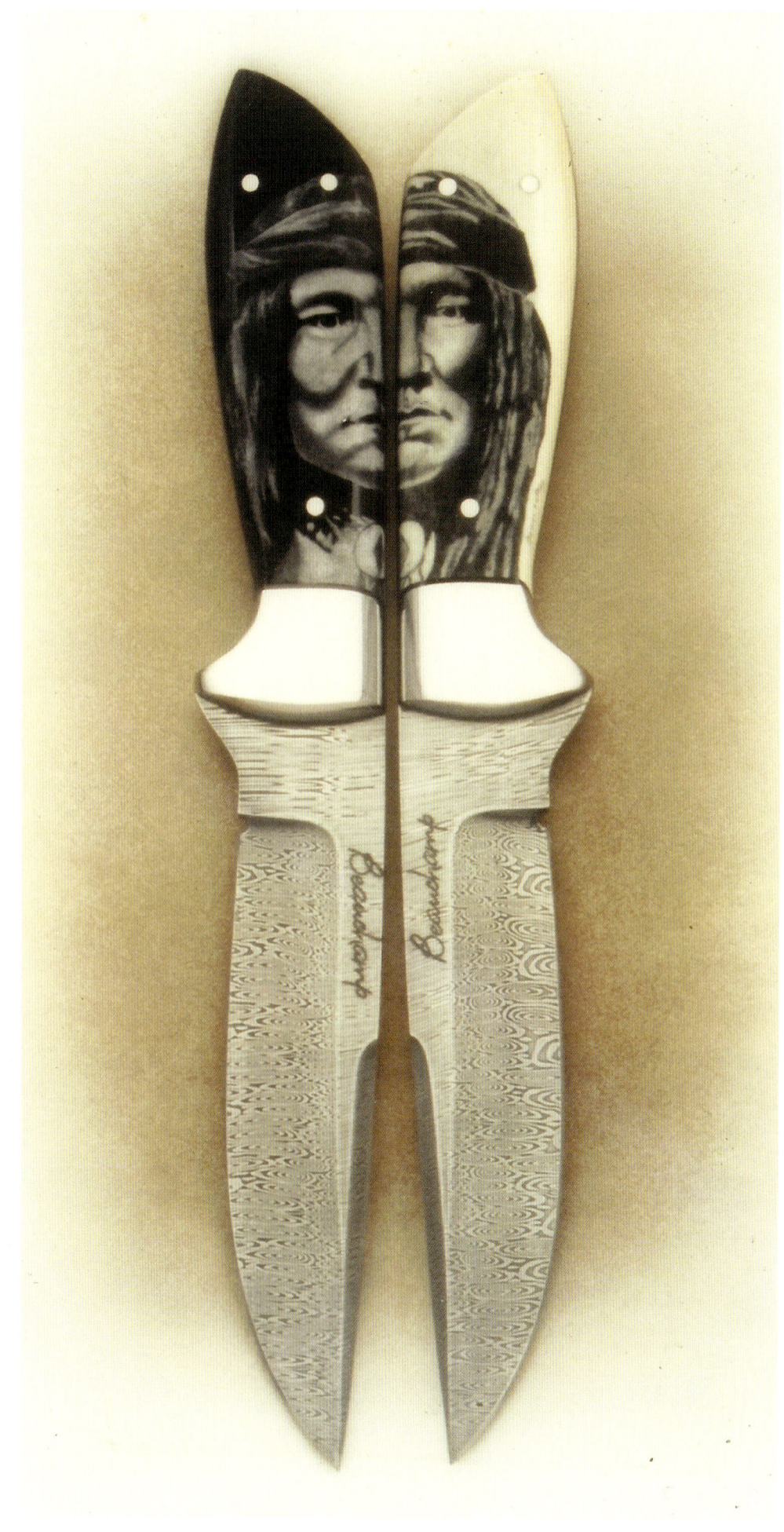

MARGARET GREENWOOD BLAKE

Margaret is a Utah native who also claims Colorado as home. She graduated from BYU with B.S. and M.S. degrees in Physical Education and Art Education. She has been a teacher, set designer, and artist for most of her life... while rearing eight children. She has been a scrimshander for twenty years and her artistic interest also includes watercolors and oils.

Scrimshaw fascinates Margaret because the materials are so unique. She loves old ivory and does most of her work on mammoth or fossilized walrus ivory. Each piece of ivory seems to have a spirit of its own which she respects and remembers as she works on each project.

SANDRA BRADY

From childhood Sandra Brady was involved in art. In high school, she learned scrimshaw, and began her lifetime career in this field. She continued her education at the University of Toledo, and at the Toledo Museum of Art, taking classes in drawing, painting, and printmaking, with particular focus on anatomy and the human form. This has allowed her to pursue the wildlife themes in scrimshaw art that she loves.

Though Sandra specializes in wildlife, her subject matter varies greatly, and her scrimshawed works range from practical, usable items, to collectible fine art pieces. Her scrimwork can be found in private collections all over the world and her work has also been displayed in the Carolina State Museum and the Art Museum of South Texas. Sandra also teaches scrimshaw, gives seminars and demonstrations, and attends trade shows throughout the country. She resides with her husband, Jim, in the Toledo, Ohio, area.

MICHAEL COHEN

Michael Cohen has been working as a freelance artist since 1973. After studying art at Cal State Northridge and U.C. Berkeley, he moved up to the Pacific Northwest and took up residence in Bellingham, Washington, where he began doing scrimshaw for the Alaska Silver and Ivory Company. Michael began marketing his scrimshaw independently in 1976, and since then has been selling his work in Alaska and Hawaii, and more recently in New England. In 2002 he won Best Color Nautical at the Mystic Scrimshanders Competition. Michael currently lives in Marlborough, New Hampshire.

Courtesy of Cindy Horovitz Wilson

BARBARA CULLEN

Originally from California, Barbara was raised in Michigan and received her Art degree from Rockford College in Illinois. She moved to the East Coast that same year and, after a museum course in scrimshaw, she began to produce pieces showing her lifelong love of animals. She uses mostly ancient ivories such as wooly mammoth, mastodon, and fossil walrus. In addition to scrimshaw, Ms. Cullen also works in the mediums of watercolor and pen and ink.

Ms. Cullen has been working as a scrimshander for over thirty years and is currently owner/resident artist of Mystic Scrimshanders in Wickford, Rhode Island. She is a winner of Mystic Seaport Museum's prestigious Award of Excellence. Ms. Cullen is founder and host of the annual Mystic Scrimshanders National Scrimshaw Competition, which draws artists and collectors from around the country.

Courtesy of Cindy Horovitz Wilson

Courtesy of Cindy Horovitz Wilson

Courtesy of Cindy Horovitz Wilson

Courtesy of Cindy Horovitz Wilson

MARK DECOU

Mark A. DeCou is a full-time, self-employed artisan, working in his woodshop located in the Rural Flinthills of Chase County Kansas. He has been working with wood and natural materials as long as he remembers. Mark's artistic training was encouraged and influenced by his father, a wood-shop teacher and master builder of hand-made furniture and clocks, and by his mother who worked with many different crafts, including sewing, wood carving, and ceramics.

Mark enjoys building Cabin and Western style furniture and furnishings, using hard woods with carved decorations, and natural materials such as deer and elk antler, steer horns, limestone, mother-of-pearl, abalone, river shell, and many other natural materials. These works include scrimshaw, powder horns, lights, tables, chairs, mirrors, and other furniture items.

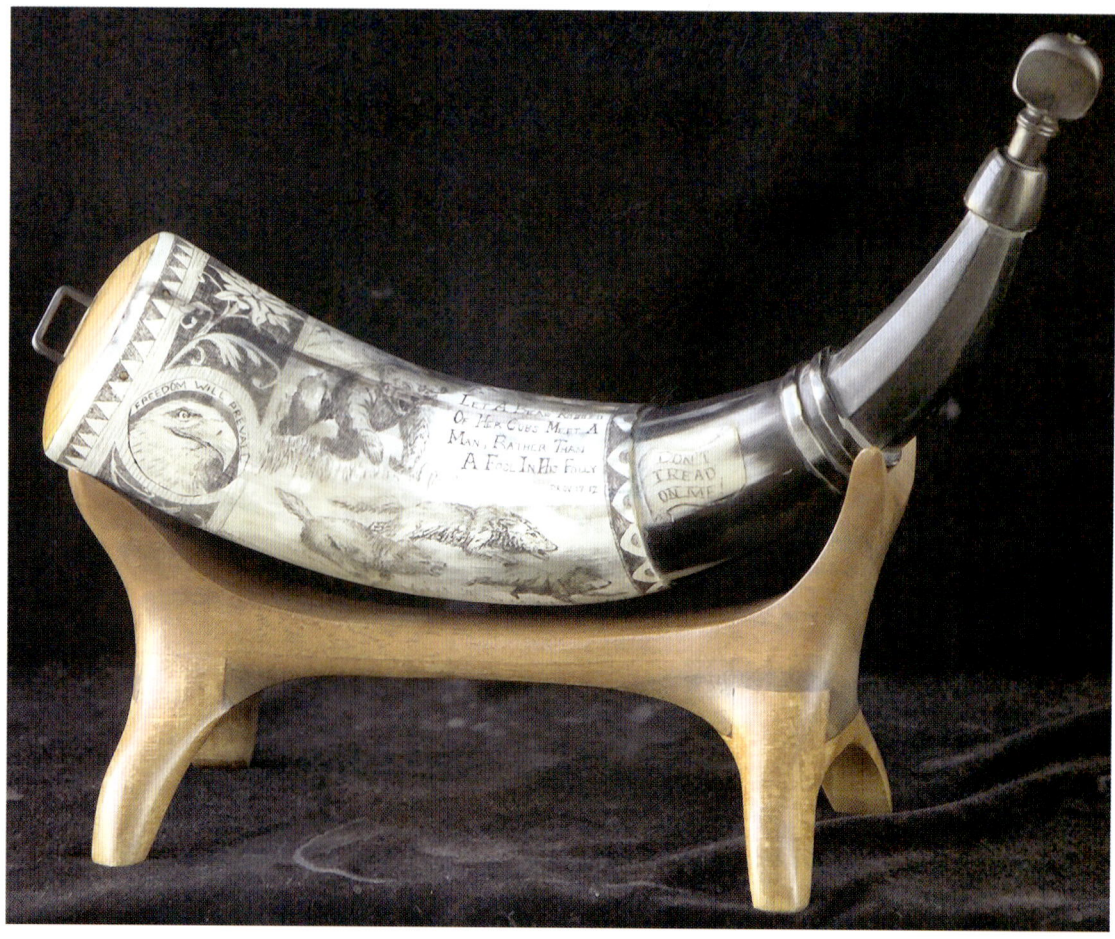

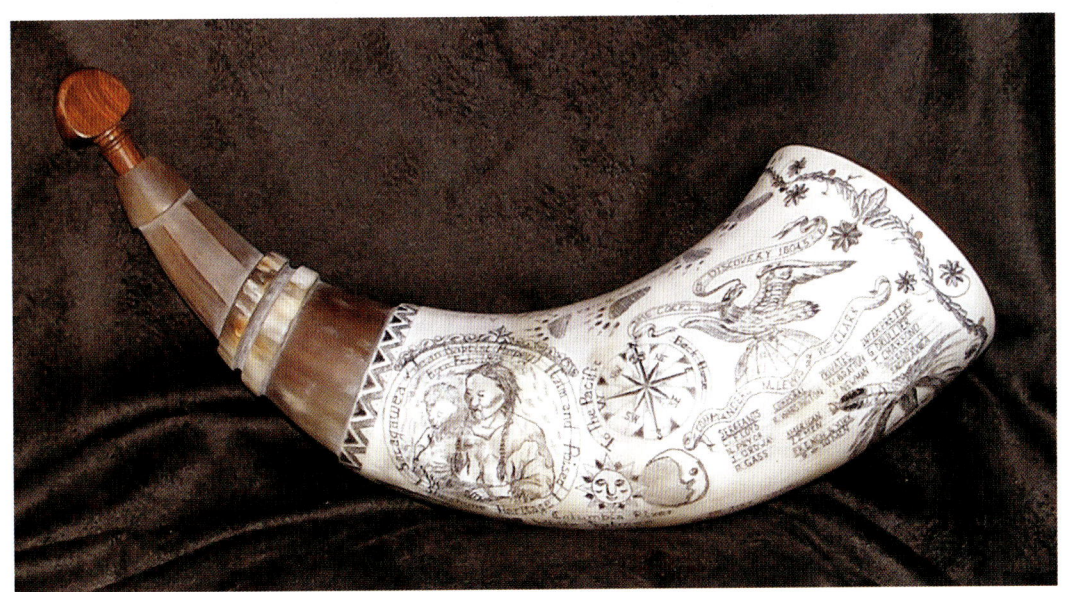

123

RONI DIETRICH

Roni Dietrich comes from a family skilled in silversmithing, lapidary, and woodcarving. Her scrimshaw reflects her love for horses, animals, and nature. In 2005, Roni won the "Best Color Wildlife" trophy at the annual Mystic Scrimshaw competition in Mystic, Connecticut. She has done scrimshaw for the world's finest knife makers and her work has been featured in *Knives*, the annual book by Krause Publications. She was also mentioned, by name, in the Tom Clancy Net Force book, *Point of Impact*, by Steven Perry.

DANIEL FARRELL

Fairly new to scrimshaw, Arizona artist Daniel Farrell is self-taught and spent many years drawing and painting portraits from life. Always having an appreciation for the clean, sharp look of steel plate engravings, he fell in love with scrimshaw in the spring of 2006. Some of his influences include Albrecht Dürer, William-Adolphe Bouguereau, and John William Waterhouse.

Working mainly on Siberian mammoth ivory, he specializes in portraits, nudes, and animals. The majority of the commissions include mermaids, sirens, and pinups on knives and poker chips and pool cues.

BOB HERGERT

Some say artists are born artists. This may be true, for by the age of 9 or 10, I was drawing in pen and ink – portraits, cars, monsters. With no formal art training, I was learning the basics of perspective and shading. A circuitous path led me to start doing scrimshaw in 1978.

I had a fun "honor" recently. A scrimshander named Bob Hergert appeared in the Tom Clancy series novels *Net Force – Point of Impact* and *Cybernation*. The author, Steve Perry, even mentioned my website, www.scrimshander.com.

I now live with my dog on the southern Oregon coast. Our town has only 1200 people and few distractions – other than its natural beauty. I serve my community by driving the ambulance. I enjoy playing guitar, camping, kayaking, photography, traveling, and "watching the stars and acting the fool."

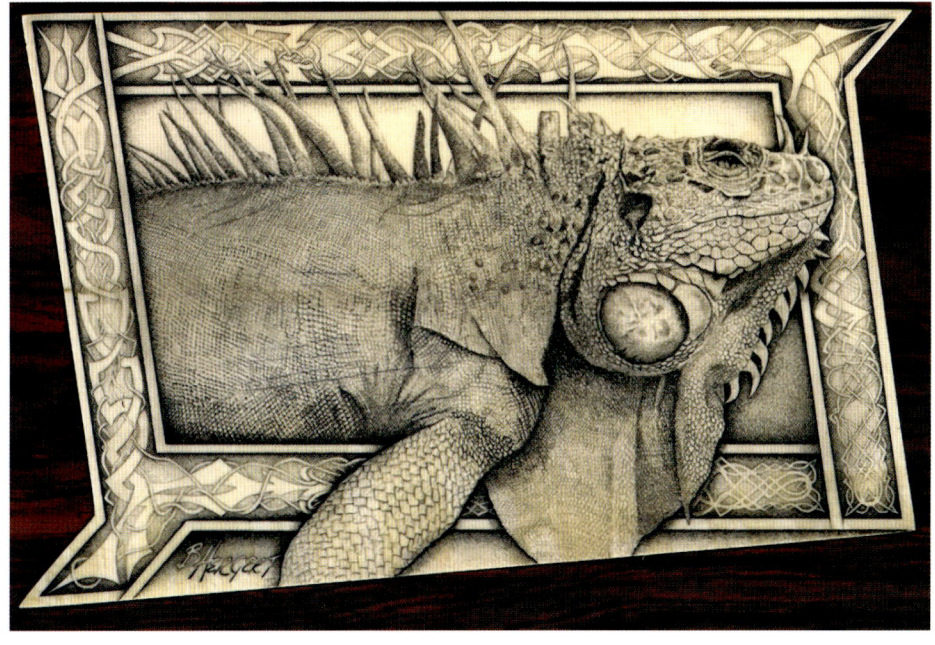

WAYNE & KAREN RENO

Wayne and Karen offer fine museum quality scrimshaw, beautiful art knives, and engraved antique firearms. Their work has been featured in several gun, knife, and art publications as well as Safari Club International. They made the first Safari Club commemorative knife honoring the Grizzly Bear. Wayne has been doing scrimshaw, engraving, and knife making since 1960 and Karen started scrimshaw in 1982.

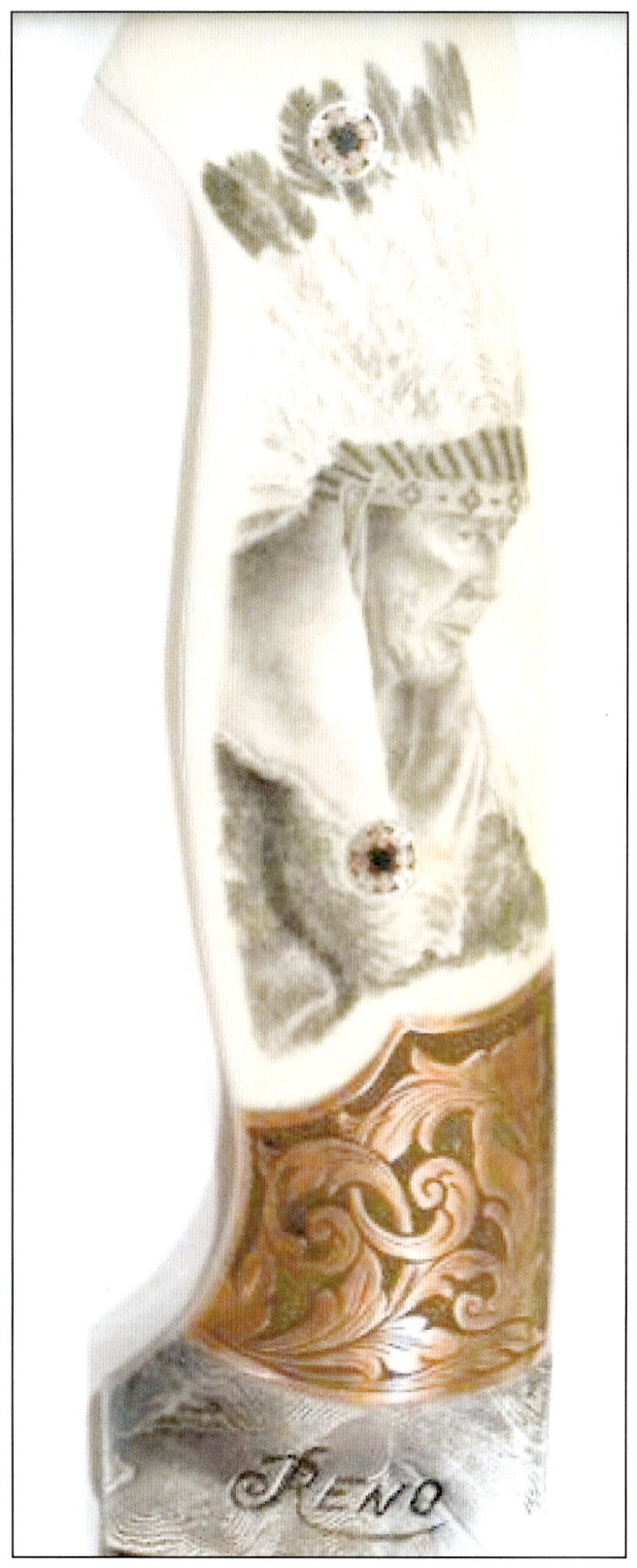

DAVID SMITH

Having spent his life in Rhode Island, nearby New Bedford and Nantucket with their old whaling history provided the motivation for David Smith launching into the art of scrimshaw. Combined with his knowledge of sailing, this background has given David an emotional commitment to traditional nautical themes, which radiate from his scrimshaw work. Each piece is created with a deep personal understanding and appreciation of the subject he depicts. Smith often makes use of photographs of wildlife or nautical scenes in conjunction with in-depth research to help create his themes.

David utilizes a stippling technique to achieve fully shaded themes on each piece he undertakes. His style of work has been described as distinctly unique from other scrimshaw, possessing a soft strength to it. He works mainly on the ancient fossil ivories of mammoth, mastodon, and walrus and prefers to use the single colors of black or sepia in his engravings to compliment the earthy brown hues often seen in these types of ivory. Between 1998 and 2006, David Smith has won twelve 1st place awards at international scrimshaw and art exhibitions for his work.

In April of 2006, David Smith was informed that the American Art Museum Library at the Smithsonian Institution in Washington D.C. has dedicated a file to the artist and his scrimshaw.

JIM STEVENS

What is most amazing about the art of Jim Stevens is that this award winning international artist is legally blind, with only a pin dot of vision remaining in both eyes. He lost his sight as a result of combat wounds suffered while serving in the U.S. Army. Jim studied art with his grandmother, Ruth Tasker, a commercial artist, as well as American master sculptor Ed Dwight and Russian master stone and gem carver Vasily Konovolenko.

Jim retired from the University of Colorado and today works as the master scrimshaw and ivory craftsman for Fenton, the international jewelry design studio based in New York City. He also teaches the art of scrimshaw and ivory inlay for the National Rifle Association's Gunsmithing School. His scrimshaw, carvings and sculpture are collected internationally and can be seen regularly at the Grand Lake Art Gallery in Grand Lake, Colorado, and the Casa de Esperanza Art Gallery in Seattle, Washington. He is frequently sought out for custom pistol grip carving and museum quality ivory and carving restoration work.

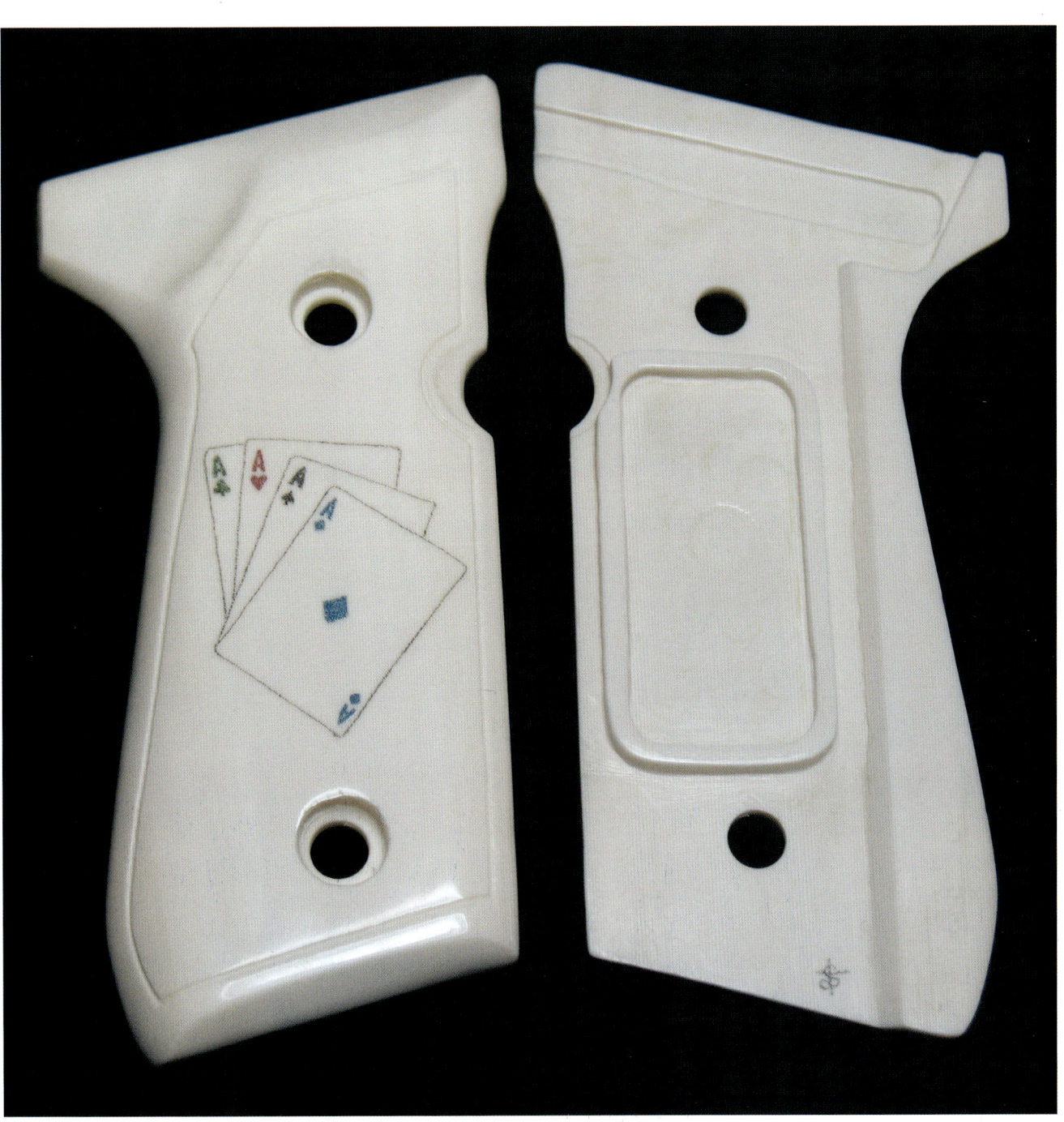

Courtesy of Anne Schneider

LINDA KARST STONE

In 1976, as an art student in Ohio, Linda was introduced to scrimshaw when hired by a local business. She was shown the basic techniques and a long-lasting career was launched. Linda pursued fine art training at the University of Toledo and the Toledo Museum of Art focusing on anatomy, figure drawing, and design.

Her scrimshaw is created using a hand-held carbide steel-tipped scribe and water color pigments. Several etching techniques bring the subjects to life. Ivory is her preferred canvas because of its warmth and personality. After more than thirty years, she still enjoys bringing the ideas, experiences, and memories of clients together with her own, to create unique art pieces.

Linda exhibits at select shows and enjoys collaborations with knife makers worldwide.

145

MATT STOTHART

I have been working in scrimshaw since 1978 when I was hired by the Alaska Silver and Ivory Company to produce scrimshaw jewelry. I quickly learned what a remarkable material ivory is to work with. It has its own inherent esthetic quality and the process of actually scratching an image into the surface makes it a very tactile art form. After a couple of years I was working on my own as a freelance scrimshander progressing from jewelry size to larger display pieces, creating scenes with nautical and wildlife themes. Generally working in color (using oil paints), my work tends to have a "painterly" style, but I do also like to work in traditional black monotone used by the original scrimshanders. The majority of my scrimshaw is on fossilized ivory, either mammoth or walrus; however, I do work on other antique ivories within the legal restrictions that appropriately apply to them.

from a sketch by Philip de Loutherbourg for "The Battle of the First of June" 1794

HOWARD L. THOMAS

Howard L. Thomas is a self-taught scrimshaw artist. He first became interested in scrimshaw while in the Navy, and spent off-duty hours studying books from the ship's library. While scrimshaw is not his only venue, it was the one art form that allowed him to put many of his other art talents into one creative palette. His great love for this style of art stems from his fascination with maritime history and his strong connection to times past. It also comes from a strong desire to leave something of himself to future generations. While many scrimshanders do the more traditional line scrimshaw, Howard prefers the more intricate detailing of the stipple technique because it offers more control in transitioning from light to dark with the shading involved in scrimshawing people, especially nudes, which are Howard's specialty. Stipple is difficult to master and time consuming, but ultimately worth the effort.

Courtesy of John Bildahl

JANE TUKARSKI

As a contemporary scrimshander, Jane's goal is to perpetuate the American folk art of scrimshaw, which is in danger of becoming a "lost art." Strict attention to detail and a mastery of painstaking engraving techniques characterize her work, primarily engraved on fossil ivory, and only with a hand held tool—she refers to herself as a purist! While pursuing a Master's Degree in textile design in Seattle, she became an apprentice scrimshander, and was immediately captivated by the challenging technique, and romance of the bygone tall ship era. Although most themes are maritime, she is also inspired by detailed portraits and nature.

As an artist member of the American Society of Marine Artists, Jane participates in maritime shows around the country, and is registered with the American Art Library at the Smithsonian. She has also had the honor of being featured on the Discovery Channel (Lynette Jennings Design Show) and HGTV.

Courtesy of John Bildahl

STEPHAN TURNER

Stephan's artistic blessing surfaced early in life. He was recognized as "the artist" as early as third grade and enjoyed that distinction throughout high school. However, things changed when he applied for art school and was rejected based on his lack of artistic maturity. He spent a year drawing and studying and was eventually accepted into the Layton School of Art and Design in Milwaukee, Wisconsin. After two years he transferred to The Academy of Art College in San Francisco, where he spent two more years majoring in fine art painting and printmaking. Printmaking prepared him for scrimshaw, which he discovered after moving to Lahaina, Hawaii.

Stephan has made scrimshaw his profession for thirty years, working for the Lahaina Scrimshaw Gallery and doing commissioned pieces for private collectors.

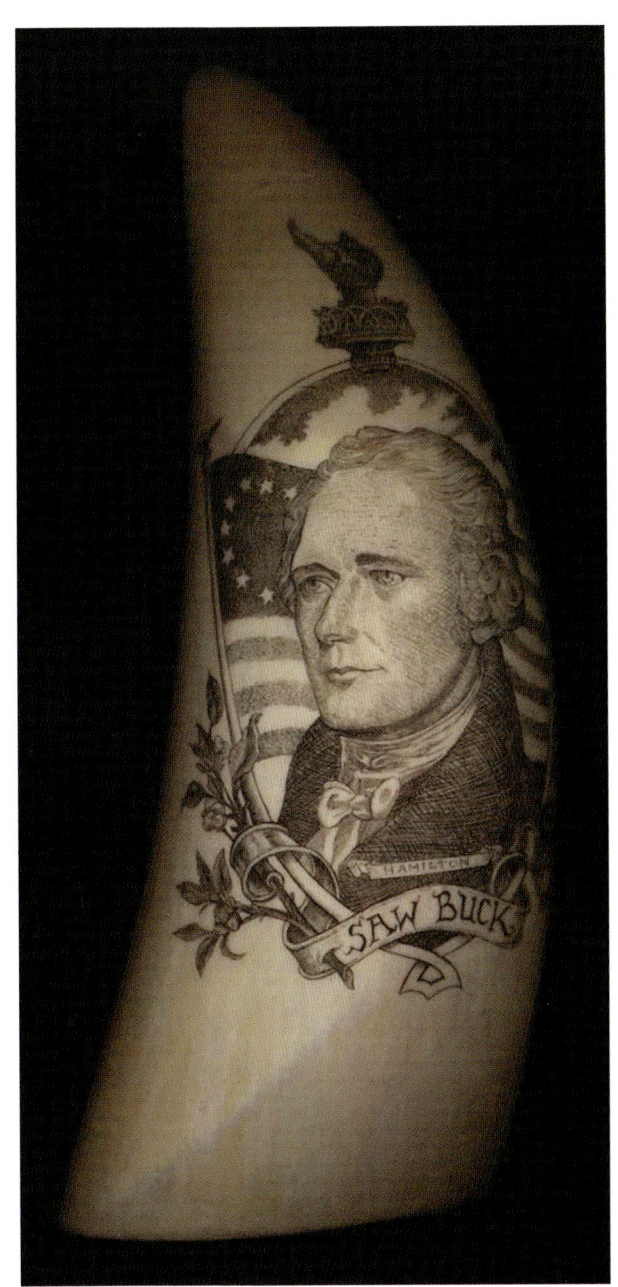

155

DAVID WARTHER II

David Warther II is a fifth generation carver of Swiss heritage living in Eastern Ohio. David's great-great-grandfather was a noted woodcarver and cabinetmaker in Thun, Switzerland, in the early 1800s. David's grandfather was a wood and ivory carver whose work inspired grandson David to enter his life's work of ivory carving at an early age.

David began carving miniature ships of wood and ivory at age six and by his teens was creating pieces for exhibit at Mystic Seaport Maritime Museum and Gallery in Mystic, Connecticut. As a teen he developed techniques to allow him to render threads of ivory, by hand, to 7 thousandths of an inch in diameter (.007 inches) to serve as rigging for his miniature ship carvings.

Currently, his collection of accurate miniature ships numbers over sixty carvings and they span the complete era of vessels under sail from 1st Dynasty Egypt (3000 B.C.) to the present day. David continues to work on his art project on a daily basis with the goal of creating 100 ships to accurately depict this history of the ship.

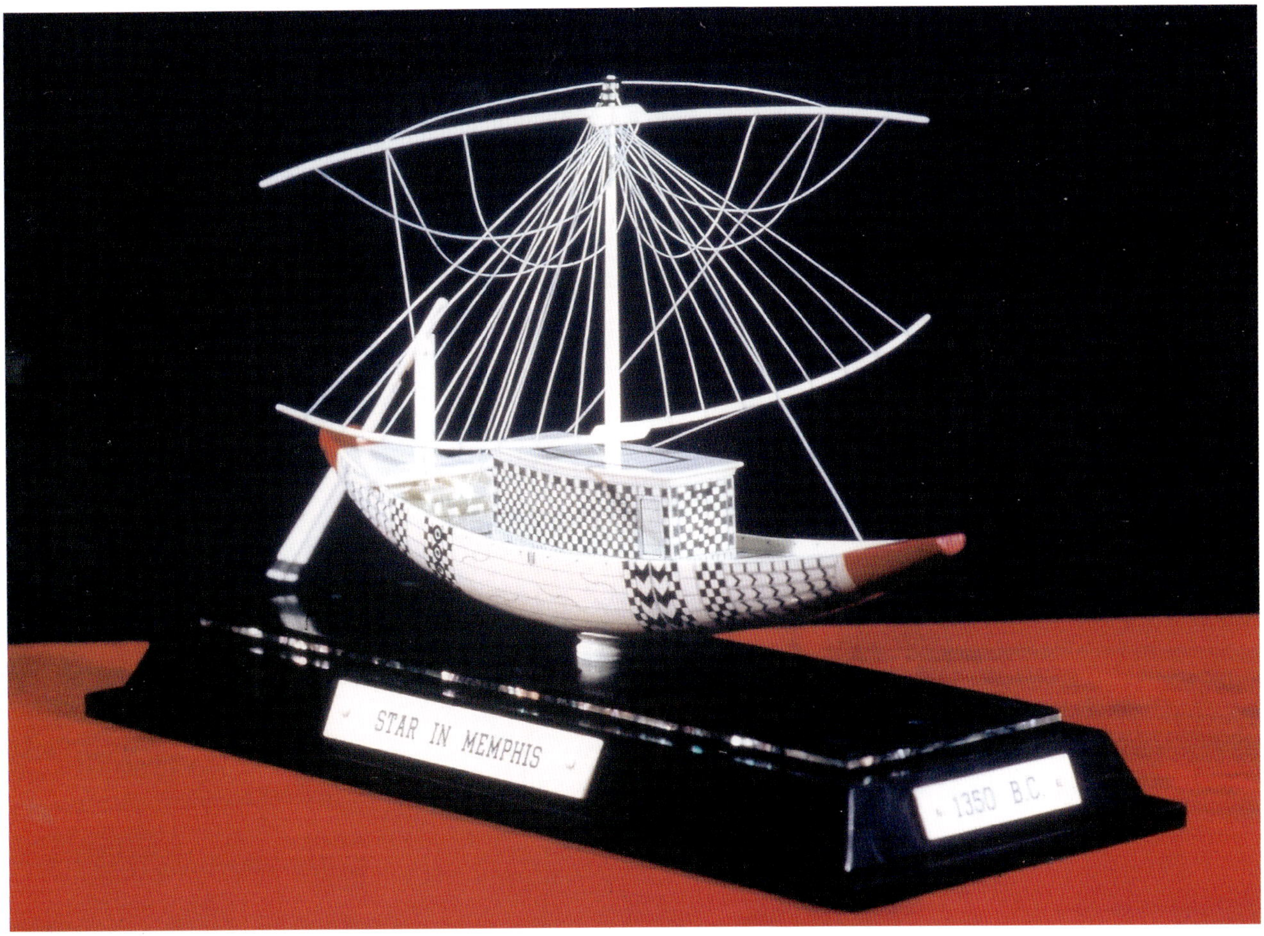

ROBERT WEISS

A native New Englander and a 1978 graduate of Pratt Institute, Bob is one of only two marine artists to have won the prestigious Rudolph J. Schaefer Maritime Heritage Award three times. This is the top award given each year at the Mystic International Marine Art Exhibition, recognizing the one work in the show that "best documents our maritime heritage, past or present, for generations of the future." He is a Fellow of the American Society of Marine Artists.

Bob has focused on creating original images through the melding of painstaking historical research and an almost painterly engraving technique.

Whether it's the drama of a "Nantucket sleigh ride," the gnarled visage of a whaling captain or the inquisitive expression of a walrus perched on arctic ice, Bob not only remains faithful to historical and natural detail, but captures the essence of his subject as well.

Appendix D: Artist Contact List

David Adams
2099 Jefferson Ave. S.E.
Apt. H-6
Port Orchard, WA 98366
Website: http:www.DavidAdamsOnline.com
E-mail: adamsonline@earthlink.net

Gaetan Beauchamp
Beauchamp Knives
125 de la Riviere
Stoneham, QC, Canada GOA 4PO
Website: http://www.gbeauchamp.ca
Email: knives@gbeauchamp.ca

Margaret Greenwood Blake
Park City Jewelry
1562 Cutter Ln.
Park City, UT 84098
Email: mgblakepc2001@yahoo.com

Sandra Brady
Scrimshaw by Sandra Brady
P.O. Box 104
Monclova, Ohio 43542
Website: http://scrimshaw-by-sandra-brady.com/
Email: sandy@scrimshawbysandrabrady.com

Michael Cohen
The Michael Cohen Portfolio
472 Main St.
Marlborough, NH 03455
Website: http://home.ne.rr.com/michaelcohen/index.html
Email: schmutz@ne.rr.com

Barbara Cullen
Mystic Scrimshanders
14 Main St.
Wickford, RI 02852
Email: mysticscrimshaw1@juno.com

Mark DeCou
Mark DeCou Studio
Wildcat Creek Rd.
RR1, Box 59
Elmdale, KS 66850
Website: http://www.decoustudio.com/index.html
Email: mark@decoustudio.com

Roni Dietrich
Wild Horse Studio
1257 Cottage Dr
Harrisburg, PA 17112
Website: http://www.roniwildhorsestudio.net/mainframe.htm
Email: Ronimd@aol.com

Daniel Farrell
2625 N. Alvernon Way, C3
Tucson, AZ 85712
Website: http://www.farrellart.com
EBay: under the User ID: danielf55

Bob Hergert
Micro-Scrimshaw
12 Greer Circle
Port Orford, OR 97465
Website: http://www.scrimshander.com/
Email: hergert@scrimshander.com

Wayne and Karen Reno
Artists of the Rockies
2808 Stagestop Rd.
Jefferson, CO 80456
Web site: http://www.artistsoftherockies.com/
Email: war@southparkco.com

David Smith
24 Peaceful Way
Tiverton, RI 02878
Website: http://www.scrimsmith.com/
Email: dsmith@scrimsmith.com

Jim Stevens
The Scrimshaw Studio
3402 N. Reed St.
Wheat Ridge, CO 80033
Website: http://www.scrimshawstudio.com
Email: stevens@scrimshawstudio.com

Linda Karst Stone
Scrimshaw by Linda Karst Stone
903 Tanglewood Lane
Kerrville, Texas 78028-2945
Email: karstone@ktc.com

Matt Stothart
Bellingham Scrimshaw
1155 N. State St.
Room #600
Bellingham, WA 98225
Website: http://www.bellinghamscrimshaw.com/
Email: mstoth@pair.com

Howard Thomas
Sailors Dream Scrimshaw
1614 St. Marys Ave.
Fort Wayne, IN 46808
Website: http:www.sailorsdream.com
Email: seasiren@sailorsdream.com

Jane Tukarski
Jane Tukarski Scrimshaw
1141 Charing Cross Drive
Crofton, MD 21114
Email: scrimshawjt@aol.com

Stephan Turner
Turner Scrimshaw
3720 Highland Ct.
Lafayette, CA 94549
Website: http:www.stepsart.com
Email: stepsart@juno.com

David Warther II
Warthers' of Ohio
P.O.Box 6
Dover, OH 44622-0006
Website: http://www.ivorybuyer.com/sales
Email: ivorybuyer@roadrunner.com

Robert Weiss
Marinearts.com
P.O. Box 58
Honomu, HI 96728
Website: http://www.marinearts.com/index.htm
Email: scrimshawinfo@yahoo.com

Bibliography

Engnath, Bob. *The Scrimshaw Connection*. Glendale, California: The House of Muzzelloading, 1982.

Engnath, Bob. *The Second Scrimshaw Connection*. Glendale, California: The House of Muzzelloading, 1985.

Flayderman, E. Norman. *Scrimshaw and Scrimshanders*. New Milford, Connecticut: N. Flayderman & Co., Inc., 1972.

Frank, Stuart M. *Fakeshaw: A Checklist of Plastic "Scrimshaw" (Machine-Manufactured Polymer Scrimshaw Fakes)*. Sharon, Massachusetts: The Kendall Whaling Museum, 1988.

Janney, Bill. *Gunstock Carving*. East Petersburg, Pennsylvania: Fox Chapel Publishing, Inc., 2002.

Robinson, Larry. *The Art of Inlay*. San Francisco, California: Backbeat Books, 1999.